September's Song

45 years of Winfield's Walnut Valley Festival

BY BOB HAMRICK

Introduction by John McCutcheon
Art Direction by Bryan Masters

Publisher: SqueezePlay Productions, LLC
Editor: Shannon Littlejohn
ISBN: 978-0-9977190-0-0
First Edition
Printed in USA

You are absolutely right.
I apologize.

Your Winfield experiences are far superior to any of the ones you'll find in this book.

The campsite you built is homier. The people around your fire are smarter and prettier. The jams are longer, bigger, better, and studded with stars. Every story told is both epic and true. And the food you cook up makes everything else look about as appetizing as a plate full of date-expired convenience store Slim Jims.

I hope you'll forgive me. I blame any shortcomings in this book on the blind men and the elephant. You know the story: Six sightless guys each try to figure out what they're standing next to based on their own perspective. They guess a lot of things. But they never figure it for an elephant.

Winfield is like that. Only instead of a handful of designated describers, this story has some 15,000 of them. And instead of an elephant, we have 14,999 of everyone else to try to make sense of.

Winfield is so far flung, so diverse that it's not even really Winfield. "The Walnut Valley Festival" is what the organizers call it.

Locals, who'd feel pretty silly saying, "We're going to Winfield" when they're already standing in Winfield, call it "Bluegrass" – or, more properly, "THE Bluegrass."

Winfield is our own, personal, one-of-a-kind elephant that is anything we want and believe it to be. It's a place where not only can anything happen, it's a place where everything will happen.

The purpose of this book is to celebrate everything that is Winfield. It's not a definitive history – far from it. It's an introduction to the delightful souls who are every bit as passionate about their Winfield as you are of yours. And who may be as close to you as the next campsite or the next seat in the grandstand.

Even though there may not be anything as grand as your Winfield in here, maybe you'll stumble onto something or someone you'd like to know more about. Maybe this'll be one more reason to come back for another one.

I hope so. After all, there's no telling just how good your elephant's gonna look next year.

Bob Hamrick, writer

3

I could barely keep my eyes open, so I didn't.

I'd had plenty of gigs I'd done over the years where I'd been exhausted before I'd started, but this wasn't one of those. No, I'd driven for nearly 24 hours straight to make this one. The supposed first flight out of Charlotte, North Carolina to Wichita, Kansas post-9/11 had been cancelled. I wasn't going to make it to Winfield. Unless I drove. Strictly speaking, unless my trusty tour manager, Tommy Slothower, drove.

So we did.

It was a particularly poignant time to drive through the purple mountains' majesty and the amber waves of grain. We drove into the heartbroken heartland of America and arrived at the Walnut Valley Fairgrounds with less than an hour to spare. So we quickly set up, I mounted Stage 2, and I sang. And, after an hour, I was tired. So I closed my eyes after intoning the first line of the best song I knew at that moment, "This Land Is Your Land." And when I opened my eyes, there stood Winfield, hands clasped and raised over their heads, a sea of loving, defiant, tear-streamed faces. And I knew there was nowhere else I wanted – or needed – to be just then. I was with these people, this festival, this family. This America.

I've played at festivals for 45 years now.

There are small intimate festivals that feel like a comfortable living room. There are enormous ones with crowds stretching beyond sight. Bluegrass, world music, children's festivals, folk festivals. There are some in which the music is a soundtrack to the beer tents and there are some in which the music is a soundtrack of our lives, of better lives. Winfield is none of the above.

Winfield is a family reunion, a gathering of the tribe, a county fair, a church social, a camporee, a folk festival the locals still call "The Bluegrass," a revival. It is a place where love affairs have blossomed and faded, where births are celebrated, deaths mourned, lives changed. I have been asked to preside over marriage proposals, christenings, and ash scatterings. Music has been seen as essential to these proceedings.

Winfield is where the rednecks and the hippies, the urbanites and the country folks, the young and the old, the rich and the poor, the locals and the out-of-towners, the Republicans and the Democrats all get along for one weekend the way we wish everyone could all the time.

In that way, Winfield is a recipe.

You take a little town with a big heart, add lots of hardworking people who bust their asses to make sure everyone is taken care of and feels welcome, mix in folks from all over the planet in love with a weird little sliver of the music world, sprinkle in performers who play that sliver, throw in a dust storm, a flood, lightning, and maybe even a national disaster. What you end up with is people caring for one another, teaching one another how to play, sharing food, building lifelong friendships. What you end up with is people taking a stranger's hand, raising it with their own into the evening sky, pulling that stranger up to stand, and joining in with a hard-earned manifesto, "This land was made for you and me."

– *John McCutcheon*

In the beginning.

Meteorologists can pinpoint exactly when lightning strikes. For the Walnut Valley Festival, the moment happened September September 29, 1972.

But long before the flash, elements that would make conditions perfect were gathering. The Beatles' "yea, yea, yeas" seen by millions on Ed Sullivan signaled a changing of the music guard. The Rolling Stones and dozens of others soon followed, bringing with them rescued songs and styles from unknown American artists – including folk singers.

After quickly becoming a mainstay on college campuses, folk – and its first cousins bluegrass and acoustic – formed the core of music festivals nationwide.

That's where a group of Winfielders come in. In 1967, Sam Ontjes was a senior at Southwestern College with some impressive stamps on his musical passport. After high school graduation, he and a friend headed for the 1963 Newport Folk Festival, whose lineup included "Doc" Watson, Mississippi John Hurt, Joan Baez, and an unknown protest singer named Bob Dylan.

Closer to home, Ontjes and a group of friends including Stuart Mossman, Jim Hale, and Bob and Kendra Redford traveled to the Mountain View, Arkansas, folk fest. After experiencing the event firsthand, it

"Coming back into the show after making sure my pickup hadn't rolled down the hill, a cop at the door asked me, 'So, how's it goin' in there?' Oh, pretty well, I told him. The music's great, and every one seems to be having a good time. 'Good,' he said. 'Keep that up and we just might let you have another one sometime.'"

– Rob Howes

wasn't long before someone asked the question, why couldn't a festival like this happen at Winfield?

With the help of Southwestern College, the answer was it could. Funded by the college but organized and administered by students, the four-day April, 1967 festival featured a handful of artists, highlighted by Jimmy Driftwood, Mance Lipscomb, and Doc Watson. "The school had given us $2,000 to cover everything," Ontjes said. "We promised Doc $700 of that, and hoped for the best."

From his viewpoint as festival director, Ontjes said a "generous guess" would put attendance for the event at about 1,500. But the door had been opened.

Fast forward to October 23, 1971, back again at Southwestern College. Musician and writer Tom James remembers showing up at the Folks Festival concert after most of the acts had finished. "When I got there, there was this clean-cut guy named Dan Crary playing fiddle tunes on a guitar, note for blazing note."

Next up on the bill was a "6-foot-5-inch New Yorker with another 8 inches of afro," James remembers. "He looked at the crowd and said, 'Man, I'd have to be a fool to follow that guy with a fiddle tune. But I don't look this way for nothing!'" And with that, David Bromberg launched into "a string of melodies both sacred and profane, sensuous and nearly senseless, active surgical removal of all twelve guitar notes so they could be reinstalled in another universe."

Then, just when it seemed Crary and Bromberg had covered everything possible as soloists, the two joined forces. "They might just as well have taken a big ol' Kansas twister down off of God's shelf and said, 'Hey, this is mine -- I forgot I left it here,'" James said.

Ontjes and his group took the success of the festival as a sign that Winfield was indeed ready and deserving of an ongoing festival. "So many people were involved back then," Ontjes said. "Of course the people who really made the festival possible were Bob and Kendra Redford. Without them putting up the money to move things to a permanent home at the fairgrounds in 1972, it would have never happened."

Non-Musician Trio
Forms Walnut Valley Association

From the Walnut Valley Occasional, January 1976

You probably couldn't find a more unlikely trio to put on a bluegrass festival. But for four years, an insurance man, a farmer, and a restaurant owner have teamed up to bring a rapidly growing and widely known festival to reality, the National Flat-Picking Championship, Bluegrass Music, Folk Arts and Crafts Festival, held each September in Winfield, Kansas.

There's another amazing thing about the three-man Walnut Valley Association – the place they chose to do the music festival. In Winfield Kansas, of all places. Not known for anything particularly out of the ordinary, Winfield perks along quite like most of the small Kansas villages of 12,000. Neither is Kansas a mecca for bluegrass fans. But Winfield is the home for two of the three WVA directors, so the Walnut Valley Festival simply leased the county fairgrounds at the west edge of town and the Flat-Picking Championship was born in 1972.

"Actually, it wasn't quite that simple," says Bob Redford, an insurance salesman who is WVA president. Bob recounts his initial involvement by admitting he didn't even know what bluegrass music was when he was approached by Joe Muret, a farmer and, at that time, an employee of the Stuart Mossman Guitar Factory. Redford recalls, "When Joe came to see me about investing in a bluegrass festival I had no idea what he was talking about. I didn't know bluegrass music from British ballads. But Joe's enthusiasm was infectious, and I became interested."

Joe Muret didn't exactly dream up the festival inspiration alone. As an employee of the Stuart Mossman Guitar Company, Joe was frequently hearing about festivals Stuart had attended. (Mossman was one of the founding directors of the Walnut Valley Association, but has been forced to give up that enterprise because of his own growing guitar manufacturing business.)

The excitement of re-telling the festival highlights seemed to Joe and Stuart to be a challenge to "some day" produce their own festival "right here in Winfield."

Eventually Joe and Stuart decided that "some day" had arrived, but were stymied by every promoter's perennial problem – money. The two decided they'd ask ten friends to contribute $1,000 each toward the first festival The first person Joe approached was Bob Redford.

At first Joe Muret was somewhat startled by Redford's response. "Why ten investors?" Bob asked. "Why not three?" Bob said he'd raise the money to finance the first festival if Joe and Stuart would do the work.

The Walnut Valley Association was formed with Redford, Muret, and Mossman as stockholders. The three talked about their goals and dreams for the festival and decided they needed a "gimmick," to attract players.

"There wasn't a national championship for

PROGRAM

FRIDAY EVENING	SATURDAY EVENING	SUNDAY MORNING
LESTER FLATT and the Nashville Grass	DOC & MERLE WATSON	GOSPEL PROGRAM
BYRON BERLINE and the Country Gazette	JIM & JESSE and the Virginia Boys	**SUNDAY AFTERNOON**
NEW GRASS REVIVAL	NEW GRASS REVIVAL	BAND CONTESTS
DAN CRARY	BYRON BERLINE and the Country Gazette	BYRON BERLINE and the Country Gazette
NORMAN BLAKE	DAN CRARY	STONE MOUNTAIN BOYS
STONE MOUNTAIN BOYS	NORMAN BLAKE	DAN CRARY
BLUEGRASS COUNTRY BOYS	STONE MOUNTAIN BOYS	and Minnie Moore

NATIONAL FLAT-PICKING CHAMPIONSHIP

FIRST PRIZE *Mossman Golden Era Custom Guitar and $500.00 cash.*
SECOND PRIZE *Mossman Golden Era Guitar and $300.00 cash.*
THIRD PRIZE *Mossman Flint Hills Custom Guitar and $100.00 cash.*

Contest Information

Be prepared to play two instrumental pieces in traditional fiddle tune or bluegrass style. Selection committee reserves the right to eliminate contestants whose selection of material and style of playing is not in keeping with the flavor of the festival.

Contestants must play only acoustical guitar. Electrified guitars will not be allowed.

Contestants must play with a flat pick. Fingerpicking will not be allowed.

You may have one rhythm guitar for accompaniment, although this is not required.

Performers billed for this festival are not eligible for the contest. All other persons, regardless of age or professional status, may enter.

Contestants must register before 10:00 a.m., Saturday, September 30, at the information booth, and pay $10 entry fee. This may be done in advance by mail if desired, by sending entry fee and name of contestant.

Be present at contest stage for instructions and designation of order at 10:00 a.m., Saturday, September 30.

Be present precisely at designated times to play. Contest begins promptly at 10:00 a.m., Saturday. Winners will play for Saturday night concert.

Judges will be selected from billed performers. In a sincere effort to approach objectivity, the following criteria will be considered be the judges, and assigned equal maximum point values:

1. Selection of material
2. Difficulty of material
3. Execution of material
4. Tuning
5. Arrangement of material
6. Showmanship
7. Overall impression of performance

BLUEGRASS BAND CONTEST

FIRST PRIZE *$300 cash*   SECOND PRIZE *$125 cash*   THIRD PRIZE *$75 cash*

Contest Information

Contestants must be prepared to do three songs, one of which is to be instrumental, the second to be vocal, and the third optional all in either traditional or contemporary bluegrass style.

All instruments in each band must be non-electric stringed instruments, th the exception of electric bass, which is optional.

Performers billed for this festival are not eligible for the contest. All other bands, regardless of age or professional status may enter.

Contestants must register before 1:00 p.m., Sunday, October 1, at the information booth and pay $10 entry fee. This may be done in advance by mail if desired, by sending entry fee and name of band.

Bands must be present at the contest stage for instructions and designation of order at 1:00 p.m., Sunday, October 1.

Contestants must be present precisely at designated times to play. Contest begins promptly at 1:00 p.m., Sunday.

Judges will be selected by the judges and assigned equal maximum point values:

1. Selection of material
2. Instrumental arrangements
3. Instrumental execution
4. Vocal arrangements
5. Vocal execution
6. Tuning
7. Showmanship
8. Overall impression of performance

anything connected with bluegrass music," Muret said. "We wanted to make the festival unique. So we issued a challenge to all guitar flat-pickers to come see who was the best, and of course, enjoy the excellent concert shows as an added bonus."

Redford said, "We were excited about that first festival, and we envisioned making a big splash on the Bluegrass scene." As fate would have it, the weather was disastrous, and so

was the attendance.

As the record cold temperatures sank on Friday in September 1972, so did the WVA directors' hopes, hearts, and budgets. The weekend included the incredible variety of weather Kansas is known for – a deep frost, later snow, then even a dust storm by mid afternoon.

"I knew Sunday morning that we were going to finish the weekend way down in the red. I was ready to throw in the proverbial towel," Redford said. But it hadn't been a complete wipeout. The small crowd was enthusiastic about the performers and they seemed to sense the potential for a really great festival. After all, nobody had ever seen three top-name performers "jam" on stage – performers who were great in their own individual rights but who had not played publicly together. If the sky had been the roof, the tiny crowd would have brought it down after Doc Watson, Dan Crary, and Norman Blake "jammed."

The WVA had suffered a financial Waterloo, but the challenge to do a festival "right here in Winfield" remained. "Besides," Redford says, "We had to try to recoup our losses."

The second festival was planned with care, and many of the lessons learned from the first festival were put to good use. But again, Kansas weather threw its torments at the hopes of the WVA.

Eighteen inches of rain soaked South Central Kansas that September, 1973. There were nine straight days of rain before the festival opened. Even though the rains continued, Redford claims, they weren't too worried. "We have a covered grandstand. We could still have had the festival in spite of the rain."

Then word came that the Walnut River was expected to flood sometime Saturday during the festival. After an emergency conference, the WVA decided to take their chances in the open, rather than cancel the festival or move it to Southwestern College. Miraculously, the rains stopped early Friday morning, and the whole weekend was shower-free. However, a few days later the entire fairgrounds were under four feet of water.

For their second effort, the WVA was rewarded with a 50% increase in attendance. The return of Watson, Blake, and Crary as a "jam special" again brought the proverbial house down. The second attempt in the festival promotion business didn't make the directors a pile of money, but it did make up a good part of the losses from the previous year.

The 1974 National Flat-Picking Championship seemed to get it all together. The weather was remarkable, the crowds were considerably larger than the 1973 edition, and the festival goers felt they had found a good thing – an annual trip to Winfield in September.

The "family reunion" feeling of the festival exists for the entertainers as well as the festival goers. As Walnut Valley publicist Art Coats explains, "We treat the performers as friends, which is exactly what many of them have become. Many of them have asked to be invited back each year. Many festival promoters go so far as to tell performers what particular songs they want to hear planed and, in some cases, how to play them. We want our performers to go out on stage and do their own thing. This philosophy has allowed us to put some things together that other festivals will never have."

"When Joe came to see me about investing in a bluegrass festival I had no idea what he was talking about. I didn't know bluegrass music from British ballads. But Joe's enthusiasm was infectious, and I became interested."

– Bob Redford, WVA President

ASSAULT ON AMERICA
Early evidence suggests bin Laden devised attacks

- Wichita Eagle, September 12, 2001

"If we can't fly, we'll drive. Winfield needs us." – *John McCutcheon*

"No, John. We need Winfield." – *Tommy Slothower, Manager*

Even Winfield changed on September 11th.

There was talk that the festival would be cancelled, that so many people in one place was too easy a target. There was fear it'd be inappropriate, gathering at a place of joy in the middle of so much sorrow. We felt guilty being there, wondering if we all needed to be watching, wondering if walking away from the broadcast flickers was to turn our backs on the loss.

But ultimately, we came home to Winfield. To grieve, to cry, to sing, to heal, and to help the healing.

"All of us there that year shared one thought, and that was that we needed to be with family. Winfield was our family that year. On Friday night, all stages, perform-

ers, and audiences sang God Bless America, simultaneously." – *Dennis Moran*

"I was camping near Nowhere when we heard the news. Out of fear I called my dad

in Missouri. He said 'Honey, Winfield is the best place for you to be.' He was right." – *Nancy G. Cook*

"Of many beautiful moments that year at

Winfield, I'll treasure The Wilders' rendition of "On the Wings of a Snow White Dove." – *Sheree Nikkel Gerig*

"At Stage 5, we passed a large flag around above our heads and there was a peaceful, respectful quiet." – *Lynne Ziegler*

"I remember standing on the hill at Stage 2 hugging my niece, and both of us just sobbing and singing." – *Mary Dell*

"Saturday, at noon in the craft pavilion, everything stopped. No one moved or spoke. I have never heard such quiet. There were two little boys running around the people, but still not making a noise. It was like everything was in another dimension. The quiet went on more than just a moment, too. Those boys did not run into anyone, and no one seemed to mind that they were doing it. They reminded us that there is life after such a tragic event." – *Lynne Ziegler*

Brian's Roses

Brian Redford was the "genuine article." So on Nov. 12, 1997, the sad news that he'd died hit the nationwide Winfield family hard.

For five years Brian, the 38-year-old son of Bob and Kendra Redford, had been director of operations for the festival. "Brian was one of those people who worked behind the scenes to make the festival go," entertainer John McCutcheon said at the time of Brian's death.

"He was the kind of person that people didn't get to know as well" as they knew others associated with the festival. "But in a thousand different ways, he typified the kind of people that really make Winfield happen.

"Perhaps like so many people who do these invisible, indispensable things, he never knew how valuable he was because he didn't get the public appreciation performers do," McCutcheon said.

"Maybe we can seize upon this sad opportunity to remember to pay respect to those people. We can do what the Carter family sang, and 'Give me roses while I live.'"

To celebrate and pay tribute to Brian's life, WVF stage signer Linda Tilton produced the "Coming Home: A Winfield Celebration" CD, featuring 17 tracks by familiar festival performers. In the album's liner notes, Linda wrote, "This collection of music is a gift of love from the Winfield festival to Gail (Brian's wife), Kevin (son), and Kayla Redford (daughter). It is a celebration of the music Brian helped to bring to us each September."

Proceeds from the CDs' sales went to an education fund established for Kevin and Kayla.

Driven

Byron Berline's band

Taking the stage at Winfield.

For 45 years, the Walnut Valley Festival has brought the best entertainers in the business to Kansas. But as with all things Winfield, the way the festival selects, books, and stages entertainment follows a formula all their own.

From the beginning, the festival's staff wanted to expose acoustic, folk, and bluegrass to an audience that may have never even heard the genres.

"This isn't the kind of event where someone in Tulsa wakes up one morning and says, 'Man! So-and-so's playing in Winfield! I gotta go see 'em,'" Trent Wagler of The Steel Wheels said. "If you come here, you're coming for the experience. And a big part of that experience is getting knocked out by some performer you didn't know existed 'til they took the stage at

Barry "Bones" Patton

13

Mark O'Connor

Norman and Nancy Blake

Winfield."

The festival's philosophy is to "book 'em on the way up." Look through the complete list of entertainers who've performed over four decades, and you'll find plenty of familiar and famous names. While some of them had big followings before they played the festival, most were unknowns when they first played Winfield.

"It's the choice they've made in musicians," Dan Crary said. "They don't spend extravagant amounts of money on the entertainers. They got people who would get audiences into the music."

14

It's not just the growing loyalty of the Winfield fans that's a plus for the festival – entertainers develop heartfelt connections to the event.

"This is a festival players want to come back to," 44-year veteran performer, judge and emcee Orin Friesen said. "It's the first event that gets inked in on the calendar each year. Anyone tries to book you those dates, it's just like the bumper sticker says: 'I can't. I'm going to Winfield.'"

"We listen when people come to us with an idea of someone they think should play the festival," Walnut Valley Association Media Director Rex Flottman said. "The people who attend here are passionate about the music. They understand the kind of entertainers that fit this place."

Entertainers themselves also help the staff scout talent. "Not only do they know which performers would do well on our stages, they know who they'd love to have the chance to share a stage with at the festival."

Sam Bush

"I'll always remember sitting in one of the guitar booths playing (and I use the term loosely) when I heard a mandolin behind me playing the same tune. So I said, 'Take it!' The mandolin exploded behind me, and when I turned to look there was Sam Bush . . ."

– *Bob Prewitt, Occasional, April 1986*

John Hartford

In The Beginning: Dan, Norman, and Doc.

From the word go, Winfield had a way of making sure the magic happened. Back at the first one in 1972, the festival did something pretty much un-

precedented at the time by putting three headliners on the same stage.

To the crowds' amazement and delight, Dan Crary, Norman Blake, and Doc Watson sat calling songs, trading solos, and backing up each other for more than an hour at the Saturday show.

"That first year was one of the greatest times of my life," Crary remembers. "I'm just this Kansas kid, just getting started, and here I am up there with my idols. And the thrill just seemed to get better every time we played."

The sessions continued for several years. Groundbreaking flat-picker and Byrds member Clarence White was booked to become the fourth guitarist in the jam, but died after being hit by a drunk driver. In his place, the festival turned to J.D. Crowe's new, young guitar player, Tony Rice.

New Grass Revival

Sign of the songs

Without ever making a sound, Linda Tilton has become one of the Walnut Valley Festival's most recognized and beloved performers. Because for 30 years, Linda has taken to the stage to artistically capture Winfield's performers' music and words in sign language.

It was a third-grade book report on Helen Keller's "The Story of my Life" that introduced Linda to the communication form. "The back of the book had illustrations of the manual alphabet, and I learned them so I could talk to my friends in class and not get caught."

In 1983, Linda earned a degree in American Sign Language Interpreting. "As I was studying ASL, I would be in my bedroom practicing sign language with the music I was listening to. Interesting that all that time spent signing to songs became the interpreting form I've become best known for."

John McCutcheon, whom she'd worked with in Kansas City, hired her for her first festival in 1986. In 1988, Bob Redford made her an official headliner with an open invitation to sign at Winfield for as long as she wanted. Linda's been here every year since.

Up on stage, she makes it look easy. But there's a lot of thought and work that goes into every song. "I spend most of my time getting ready for a performance by studying the lyrics," Linda said. "English has a different sentence structure, slang and idioms than ASL, so I need to pay attention to the message that the performer has written."

But the songs she interprets at Winfield are far more than lyrics – they're melodic, rhythmic stories that must be communicated for the audience. "If I was signing but not showing the musicality through my body and signs, the deaf audience wouldn't receive the full idea that the musician intends them to have."

From a secret language only her grade-school friends could understand to telling unheard stories to thousands, Linda Tilton has turned her passion to communicate into a powerful, lyrical art form that fills the silence. She tells the story of Winfield beautifully.

Putting talent to the test.

What began as a savvy marketing ploy has turned out to be the heart and soul of the Walnut Valley Festival.

Against the backdrop of an increasing national obsession with acoustic music in general and bluegrass in particular (thanks to Bonnie, Clyde, and Earl Scruggs) the founders of the Walnut Valley Association wanted something that would make their festival, well, different.

Every gathering had bands. Most had parking lot jamming. But nowhere were there contests, or championships. And so, the powers at Winfield created the National Flatpicking Championship.

From the start, the play-off was so central to the festival that the weekend was officially named "The National Guitar Flat-Picking Championship, Bluegrass Music and Folk Arts and Crafts Festival."

Banjo, fiddle, fingerpicking, autoharp, and mountain and hammer dulcimer contests were added to the mix, and soon Winfield was a must-attend contest event for some of the finest players across the nation and around the world.

The list of contest winners reads like an acoustic music's who's who. Mark O'Connor, Stephen Bennett, Steve Kauffman,

teenager Alison Krauss, and 12-year-old Chris Thile (pictured center, page 22) are just a few of the most notable names dropped. (You'll find a complete list of top finishers in every competitive division in the back of this book.)

For every winner, there are dozens who come up short – some of them year after year.

"I've entered six years in a row, and I've never made it to the top three," one participant said. "Of course I want to win, and I'm still convinced I will someday. But even when I don't, I know all the work I do to have a shot at Winfield makes me a better player than I ever could be without being here."

A few years after the festival began it was decided Winfield wasn't a beauty contest – it was a beautiful music contest. And so windowless, soundproof rooms were created to isolate judges from anything other than the notes.

Judges themselves are some of the best on their instruments, chosen from the field of performers at that year's festival, or from regional-national musicians known as powerhouse players.

Before the start of the competition, three judges and one alternate are closed in the booth. Stage announcers refer to the contes-

"You're on the stage – sweat trickling down your forehead, hands won't stop shaking, and you're thinking that right now you'd rather be in a dentist's chair. So, is the chance of winning worth all the agony, frustration and nervousness? In a word, yes."

– Bill Bryant, Autoharp

"This is the Wimbledon of American acoustic music."
— *Eric Lugosch,*

"Winning at Winfield is a credential that lasts a lifetime."
— *Pete "Dr. Banjo" Wernick*

"The first year I won, I'd buy one of those big turkey drumsticks, pull my sleeve up over my hand, and walk around the fairgrounds gnawing on it. I'd hear people say, 'Why is that girl who won the fiddle contest eating her hand? She's not going to win next year if she keeps that up!'"
— *Alison Krauss*

tants by numbers only. During the competition, judges keep their own scorecard until each contestant has played. After the numbers are shared, the judges agree on five contestants to compete in the second round. From that group, three are chosen as their division's winners.

"These contests are a joy to be a part of," one judge said. "Usually there are a few players who just really stand out from the crowd, so most times we come to the same opinion."

Winning Winfield is a big deal. Everyone who places is awarded a new, top-of-the-line instrument, trophy, and title. That's important to performers working to break out of the amateur ranks and into full-time performing and recording.

"Things just opened up for me after I won in Winfield," a winner said. "After that, the people at my shows didn't necessarily know my name. But they knew I was good enough for Winfield, and that was more than enough for them."

How Does The Song Go?

Kelly and DonnaMulhollan will admit the event they host at Winfield sometimes feels like "an orphan child of the festival."

Every year, the husband and wife duo, who perform musically as Still on the Hill, co-host two sessions of the Walnut Valley Festival's NewSong Showcase to honor the best of hundreds of original songs.

Too often, that songwriting talent gets overlooked. "Winfield's the ultimate camping festival," Kelly said. "It's the ultimate jamming festival. But it's not the ultimate songwriting festival. Not yet."

Still, there's a welcoming, laid-back feeling at Winfield that encourages writers to compete in the showcase. "This isn't a Kerrville Folks Festival where jamming and playing along on someone else's song is frowned on. That's cold and joyless compared to here. That's why Winfield's Showcase is growing."

Donna and Kelly have hosted the Showcase since they inherited the job from the event's founders Crow Johnson and Ernie Hill. Over the years, the showcase has grown to include more than 300 entries in 10 different categories. Awards are presented for category winners and runners-up the Thursday and Saturday of the festival.

"I'm always amazed by the quality of songs people enter," Donna said. "Across the board, in every category, the songs are meaningful, they're well-crafted, they tell a story."

"People are writing songs for what I consider the right reason – for the love of it," Kelly added. "We don't get a lot of people who are trying to nail a Nashville hit. There's not a lot of gimmickry. We hear songs that were written out of necessity. I hope it stays like that."

The toughest part of the job is finding judges. "People think Kelly and I judge the songs," Donna said. "That's just not true. We know so many of the contestants, it wouldn't be fair."

While there are no set criteria for judging, Donna and Kelly look nationwide for people who fit a definite profile. "We want someone who's passionate, who'll take the time not just to listen to a song, but who'll be able to identify strengths and weaknesses," Kelly said. The judge's comments for each song are mailed to the writer.

"Not everyone who enters is going to win," Donna said. "But everyone is going to learn something. Even if you don't win we want you to get something out of this. Hopefully, something that will help make you a better writer."

Newsongs Showcase Categories

- Winfield
- Children
- Religion/Spirit
- Feelin' Blue
- Instrumental
- Sweet Memories
- Love Songs
- Better World
- Humor
- None of the Above*

*Donna's advice - Be careful of this one. Year after year, it's the category bulging at the seams with entries. And Kelly reminds you to always be sure to check the disc you're entering on more than one player. "Too many songs haven't been judged because the disc wouldn't play."

Confused? Get in line.

Here's the only thing you need to know about Land Rush: No camper in the history of the Walnut Valley Festival has ever figured it out. In fact, the process leaves a lot of Walnut Valley officials at a loss for words as they try to explain exactly how it works.

The event takes its name and some of its drama from the Oklahoma Land Runs of the late 1800s as settlers tried to grab a piece of homestead land by getting to it first. "Before we started Land Rush, we had people lining up their campers and trailers along US 160," Rick Meyer, Coordinator of Special Events for the city of Winfield said. "The police asked us to do something about it, so we opened up the fairgrounds to give early arrivers a place to wait."

Land Rush was started so that everyone could have a fair chance at getting a good camping spot. "Nowadays, people are more concerned about getting electricity for their camp than they are the campsite itself," Meyer said. Campers start pulling into the fairgrounds as early as mid- to late-August. Though they'll ultimately camp in either the West or Pecan Grove, vehicles park in lines in a huge area in front of the grandstand.

Day by day, the mass of wheeled aluminum grows, until the grounds become a sea of white tin. A month before the festival officially starts, Line Rush (or "pre-Land Rush line-up") starts, with a lottery for first Land Rush numbers. Starting at 7 a.m. nine days later, Land Rush numbers are handed out to new arrivals, and taped inside car and truck windows like a badge of honor.

One week before the festival, on a Thursday at 6 a.m., thousands of engines fire up, chairs set in a circle for last night's jam are stuffed anywhere they'll stay put. People check their watches (again) and whisper the Land Rush prayer – "Oh, God, please let my engine start!" Meyer drives his John Deere Gator up to the lowest number in line, nods slightly, and the first Titanic-sized camper rolls out. One by one, he moves down the line as anxious campers follow each other like schoolkids on a field trip.

Once they've reached the campgrounds' borders, lines dissolve and expand every which way. "It's chaos," one longtime Land Rusher said. "But it's Winfield chaos, and that's good."

Meyer has a few suggestions for first-time participants. "Know what you're in for. It's a good idea to watch this thing as a bystander before you make a commitment to get in line." And finally, Meyer's most important suggestion: "Come take over my job so I don't have to do it."

Long before there was Winfield the festival, there was Winfield the town.

Founded in 1870, the community is named for Rev. Winfield Scott – who shrewdly promised to build the town a church if they'd give him naming rights.

For a lot of festival goers, this city of 12,000 has a special small-town charm to it. It's the kind of place you want to come back to – even if you don't always live there.

"We're good at being hosts," Winfield City Manager Warren Porter said. "It's fun to live in a place where people look forward to coming to your community."

But even welcomed visitors that suddenly double the population put a strain on the community. "Almost everyone I know stocks up so we won't have to go to the grocery store during Bluegrass," bank officer Teresa Bradbury said. "There are just too many people."

"It's hard to put a dollar figure on what the festival means to Winfield economically," Porter said. "But we estimate it brings in about 1.5 percent of our taxable income.

"It's not enough to make a community, but it's a good source of revenue. And for small, locally owned businesses, Bluegrass is a second Christmas."

Leon & Markie's Not-To-Be-Followed Advice For WVF Newcomers

1. Where to camp. You don't want to miss out. Ask to camp in the Pecan Grove. It is the only cool place. The West Campground is full of tone deaf oldies in big motor homes; they do their picking inside where you cannot hear them or join in.

2. You don't need an electric hookup; the weather is always fine so there is never a need for heat or AC. You don't want to look like a sissy camper, do you?

3. When to arrive. All the stuff about Land Rush is just a few perfectionist, OCD people who want to make a contest about everything. Friday is plenty early. Don't waste your time.

4. The people with fancy decorated camps and lots of players are not really having more fun than you. They just pretend to have more fun and more friends.

5. Although the porta-potties may look and feel as if they might turn over, do not fear, they always remain upright.

6. If you like to get to sleep early, then the Pecan Grove is the place you want. The generators on all the big motor homes in the Main Campground will keep you awake.

7. If you have a small tent, feel free to set it up in front of that old truck they call "Stage 5." It is really neat to get to know the Stage 5 folk, and this is a great way to meet them.

8. Nudism is only allowed near the Horse Barn in the big parking lot. There are fewer trees to bother the nude sunbathers.

9. If you like a little practical joking, try cutting down the parachutes at about 6 a.m.

10. The best practical jokers at the festival are the clowns who ride around in the used police cars. Just throw your drink on them or make an obscene gesture toward them. They pile out of those cop cars like Keystone cops and run all around. A fun sight for sure.

- Markie (the short one) and Leon (the one with a full beard)

Editor's note: It's a joke. Okay?

"What we've got here is tents
– hundreds, thousands of
tents – campers, campfires,
lanterns by Coleman and
various elves, glow-in-the-
dark kids zipping around
like whirly-gigs in the oak
and pecan groves.
Little communities of friends,
families amid the scattered
sun showers, banners,
porta-potties, trikes and
bikes, roasted marshmallows,
roadkill stew. People milling
around like a grand family
reunion."

– Susanne Page

Winfield camping isn't exactly "roughing it."
Look around, and you'll see sites filled with all the comforts of home and then some. Complete kitchens, easy chairs, sofas, coffee tables, floor lamps. Because the ultimate goal is not to "get back to nature." It's to get back to Winfield.

What's in a name?

What's in a name? A whole lot of everything if it's the name of a Winfield campsite. It's probably safe to say the name started as some snort-provoking joke and quickly became sacred. So don't spend a whole lot of time or brain cells trying to figure them out. As one site's name suggests, "Shut Up and Camp, They Explained."

2 Much Stuff	Fiddle Fest	Ovarian Woods
3 Trees	Flaming Duck Farts	Penguins
Albert Hall	Flood Stage	Pepper Jam
Autoharp Junction	Flood Victims	Pickin' Parlor
Band Camp	Fork In The Road	Pink Elephant
Barry Bones	Froggy Mountain	Plague Camp
Bentley/Stout	Front Porch Radio	Posse Family
Bluegrass Chicks Rule	Girls Gone Winfield	Pumpkin Creek Pickers
Bucket Camp	Glitter Gulch	on Pickers Point
Budman	Grassholes	River Rats
Buller/McIntosh	Greenhorns	Roe Family
Buzzards Roost	Grenola Camp	Rollin R Farm
Cajun Willow	Hammerhead Gang	Rookie Stop
Camp Avalon	Harpie NeoCamp	Scamp Camp
Camp Brigadoon	Herbie Husker/Simcox	Shut Up & Camp They
Camp Cock	Hog Pen	Explained
Camp Hilton	Inner Hillbilly	Snow/The Hole
Camp Kamo	Joke Camp	Spoon Camp
Camp Super Pickle	Geezers of Anarchy	Stillwater
Camp Whatever	Kamp Konze	Summer Camp
Carp Camp	Kenny Cornell	Taylor/Thornhill
Chicken Train	Mary & Geoff	Tent Farm
Comfortable Shoes	Muddy Acres	Thistle Dew
DeWayne Brothers	Neon Guitar	Total Hogs
Moi-De-Do Area	Nighttime Drives	Watering Hole
Dulcimer Alliance	Me Crazy	Waukiweinn
Dylan D.	Next to Nowhere	Wild Bill
Farley Valley Assoc.	One Fret Away	Wood-N-Head
Fast Food Junkies	Outback	Yellow Canoe

STELLA!

Here's the true story of why Winfielders yell STELLA. (Or, at least, it's one of the true ones.)

In 1974, on a terribly windy night, a young woman who'd just won the finger-plucking contest spent the rest of the day celebrating.

By that night, as her campmates set out to make the rounds, the woman was so tired she could barely stand. To keep her safe, they tied her belt loops to the camp's WWII surplus parachute.

For a while, she slept peacefully even though a big storm was threatening. As her friends ran back to the camp, a huge wind picked up, with a gust bigger than anyone could remember. Within seconds, the parachute came untethered, dragging the poor finger-plucker up into the sky.

As she sailed off, her distraught friends cried out for her. "STELLA! STELLA!," they pleaded. But she was never seen or heard from again. That's why, to this day, Winfield campers holler out STELLA in hopes of finding their long-lost champion.

- Lance Jungmeyer

Virgin Territory.

For the inner introvert who's hiding out in all of us, the thought of stepping into the middle of 15,000 very strange strangers is sure to set off alarm bells. But, for better or worse, no one at Winfield stays an outsider for long.

One of the festival's greatest traditions is its treatment of first-time attendees. "Virgins," they're called. And once word gets around that there's one in the area, a fresh celebration breaks out.

Winfield's version of the red carpet is a white T-shirt with the word VIRGIN scrawled across it in magic marker. Wearing this walking billboard, the festival newcomer is recognized and treated as royalty wherever they go.

Festival veterans waste no time welcoming and educating the new kid. "Where you need to go and what you absolutely gotta do" are the most often shared bits of information – though a few mischievous souls will offer misinformation. Best advice of all is, if you have a question, just ask. We've all been where you are before. And we've all come back for more. Show up once, and you're one of us.

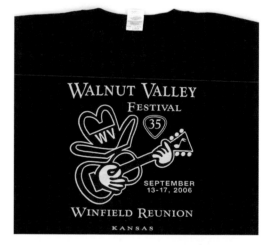

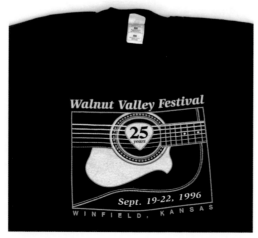

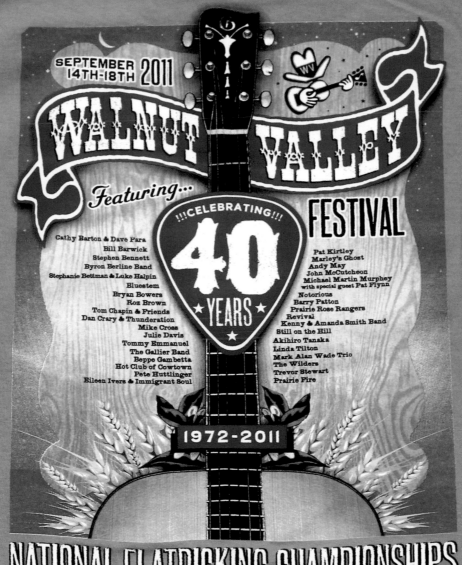

Gathering in the groves.

One of the first things someone at the ticket office is going to ask you when you pull in to camp is, "Pecan Grove? Or West Campground?" Be careful how you answer. It can make all the difference.

Let's start with the closest site to the ticket trailer. West Campground is also known as "the Walnut Grove." A third option is "Hollywood."

That upscale, la-dee-da title comes from the massive number of swanky RVs that populate the camping area. In fact, that used to be the only place you'd find camping trailers in Winfield. Because the other camp area was reserved strictly for tents.

That area's the Pecan Grove. It has pecan trees, in groves, so the official name isn't quite as contentious. Still, in keeping with the West campground's Hollywood, the Pecan Grove's often been labeled "Hooterville."

Old-timers remember being able to stand in the middle and see both ends of the Pecan Grove just by looking over the pup tents. Then, a lot of the hippies got old. And achey. And decided a tin shed on wheels with beds, heat and air conditioning, and indoor plumbing wasn't all that bad. And before long, RVs swarmed in like locusts.

People will try to match camper personalities to the places they camp, and there may be some bit of truth to that. Still, we're one community, one big happy family. Hooterville or Hollywood, it's all Winfield.

Walk as far south from the Bennett/Colby camp as you can without falling in the river and you'll find yourself under the cover of the biggest parachute you've ever seen. You're in Rat Camp, a quirky, one-of-a-kind institution that could only happen in Winfield.

"We consider Rat Camp to be the reception area of the grand hotel – that just happens to be a bunch of pecan trees," Gail Haywood-Tucker said. Haywood-Tucker (aka, Katie Redstar) is one of four original River Rats who first set up the camp in 1989. Others include her husband, Greg "King Rat" Tucker, Paul Hagemeier, and Tom Haver.

The story behind the name is a kind of Alice's Restaurant with a Kansas twist. As the guy hauling Gail's trash started making increasingly less frequent stops, the clutter piled up and word in rodent world that the buffet line was open spread quickly.

As Greg set out to rid the place of varmints he also began studying books on taxidermy. Before long, he'd fashioned himself a tulip rat-skin hat. "He sported it proudly," Nanetta Bananto wrote in a poetic ode to the camp, "but failed to consider that sweat made his rat hat smell just like a rat."

The next year, Greg tore the hat apart and made 13 buttons to hand out to people who found their way to the River Rat Camp, and the gathering began to create traditions and take on all the characteristics of a festival within a festival.

Each year has its own rat-based theme. The Wednesday of the official festival, hundreds of Winfielders grab a lawn chair and show up under the parachute for a full schedule of everything rat. Inventive, varminty costumes are displayed and judged. And impromptu bands compete for the coveted River Rat Band Scramble trophy.

Bands are formed from randomly drawn names. The four- or five-member groups are given a short time to get to know each other, write a theme-related song, and rehearse for the afternoon's battle of the rats.

"You don't have to be a musician to play in the Band Scramble," Gail said. "You can have broken eardrums, and you're still welcome. This camp is all about inclusion."

At times, the joy of River Rat Camp has known tears. In 2008, Gail's son K.C. died in a freak accident. "He was always a part of my Winfield. I knew that no matter how far apart we lived I was going to see him there." In remembrance of him, the camp has planted several trees and flowers in the grove.

"There is so much love at this camp and this festival. Winfield is where my family is. This is where I grew up."

One of the oldest campsites in Winfield, Stillwater Camp has more traditions than they can possibly remember. Since 1975, the core of the camp is made up of people who either live in Stillwater, OK, went to school at Oklahoma State University or stumbled into the camp at some time and never found their way out.

The camp's banner is crafted from purple Crown Royal bags. There's an army tent large enough to host a national political convention.

In times past, Stillwater campers brought pickup loads of used dorm and apartment furniture, both to comfortably enjoy during the festival and to torch in a huge bonfire to signal the festival's end.

But that's a thing of the past, as either fire regulations got tighter or the Stillwater camp participants got more responsible. You decide.

Walk as far north from the Rat Camp as you can

and you'll stumble into a campsite that may be a little less chaotic but every bit as magnificent and joyous as its festival cousins to the south.

Like a lot of things in Winfield, this Walnut Grove institution answers to two names. For friends and family of Wichita's first family of acoustic music, the camp is the home of the Bennett Brothers. For others, the site's known as a home base for the group that stages Colby's Pickin' on the Plains Bluegrass Festival each year. After camping next to each other for a few festivals, the Bennett and Colby contingency decided they had too much in common to stay separate, and merged into a single camp.

Their area's defined by a huge expanse of circled RV wagons, and a multiple tent-covered common area. In addition to stacks of folding chairs, the place is dotted with sofas, easy chairs, coffee tables, and floor lamps that give it a welcoming living room feel.

The Bennett/Colby camp attracts the best players and singers at the festival, and always has. "Back in '82 when the camp started, a lot of bands really centered on instrumentals, and picking," Sedgwick County district attorney and bass player Marc Bennett said. "My uncles, on the other hand, really loved

to sing. I think a lot of performers and camp players got tired of picking all the time and stopped by our place for something different."

Today the camp is likely to be filled with 40 or 50 top-notch players who've traveled across the country specifically to get to this jam. The jam is seldom at a lack of a song to call, or at a loss for lyrics of the most obscure song.

"Everyone seems to be at their best when they're playing here," Bennett said. "There's a lot of support for each other. There's a genuine appreciation of good playing, and so (they) work to stretch it out a bit."

The camp has always been all-age friendly, and older players often clear the chairs for kids to show what they've got. "People always got a kick out of hearing the young McLemore Twins – Blake and Brandon – play. Now that they've grown up and have their own band, Driven, they're less of a novelty and have become a huge draw."

Making music at the camp builds family, Bennett said. "I consider every one of the people here very close family. When one of our kids gets married, we all go to the wedding. When someone passes, we all show up for the funeral. You get to the place where you just enjoy the experience when you can, and you get everything out of each year that you can."

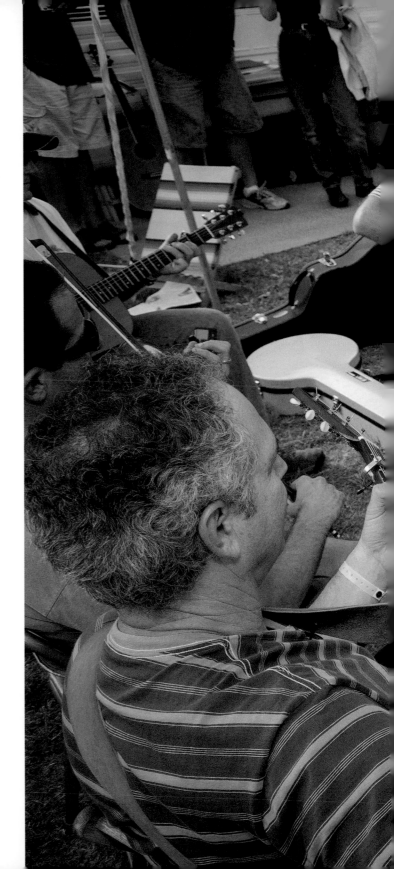

Winfield is a wonderland for the senses. Songs and strains of songs mix, and melodies shift with every step you take. Bacon sizzles, ribs slow-roast, burgers grill with scents that dance and twirl with wood smoke. And in the darkness millions of lights are glowing, pulling you forward to someone's idea of heaven, welcoming you to come on in, if you're so inclined.

Playing the last set of the festival in the grove, Beppe Gambetta asked the first 10 rows to move so he could teach everyone to tango. It wasn't pretty or quick, but people finally stumbled out of the way. Beppe handed each man a rose stem to hold between his teeth, and the crowd danced the festival away.

Strangest question WVA receptionist Paulette Rush has ever been asked: "How can I get an emergency call while I'm at the festival waiting for a transplant?"

For people of the Jewish faith, Sukkot is the autumn celebration of the temporary, marked by the building of a short-term shelter filled with the things that truly matter. Family. Friends. Food. Drink. Music. Joy. Gratitude. Hope. Here, most everybody calls it Winfield.

People smile because other people give us something to smile about. People laugh because other people say and do funny things. People hurt. And people help to heal.

The connections made at Winfield go far beyond fair-weather friends. They begin through shared, deliberate experiences. They're tempered by challenges and cooperation. They grow into relationships in which others know us better than we could ever know ourselves. Those Winfield connections, those friends, are there for us. At the festival, and throughout the year. They help us to smile. To laugh. And to heal.

Sometimes it seems the only thing we have in common at Winfield is Winfield. Lawyers and hog farmers sip from the same Mason jar. Hippies and rednecks grin ear-to-ear, side-by-side. There's a sense of self and an appreciation of others. So, if you have to put a face on Winfield, just draw a smile. And leave it at that.

It's a question for the ages:
Does Winfield let you pretend
to be someone you're not?
Or does it give you the all-clear
to discover who you've always
really been?

That "circle of life" thing is in full force at Winfield. Couples meet, fall in love, marry, and make room in their camp for baby bluegrassers. Many believe there's no more beautiful way or place in which to begin life together than by exchanging I-dos under Winfield's lush green cathedral ceiling.

"Come wedding time, everyone was decked out in their finest tie-dye, with the bride in as white a dress as the festival mud would allow. The bride glowed, the preacher blessed, and the band sent the married couple away with a rousing 'How Mountain Girls Can Love.'"

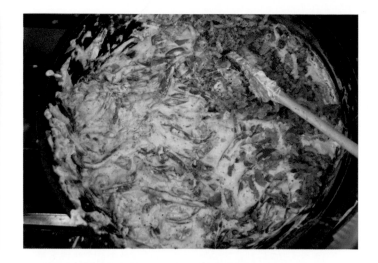

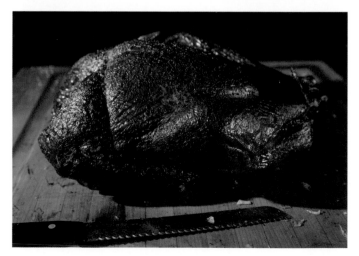

"I first came in 1991. And from the moment I got there, I felt as if I had been taken up in an alien spaceship. The spaceship dropped me off in the Pecan Grove and my life was changed. No phones, no TV, no newspapers. Just laughter and music for four days. My group camped next to some people from Oklahoma that year and we have camped together every year since. We have visited each other in our homes, watched our children grow up, and shared good times and hard times with each other. I have not missed a Winfield in 25 years."

– *Leah Bonebrake*

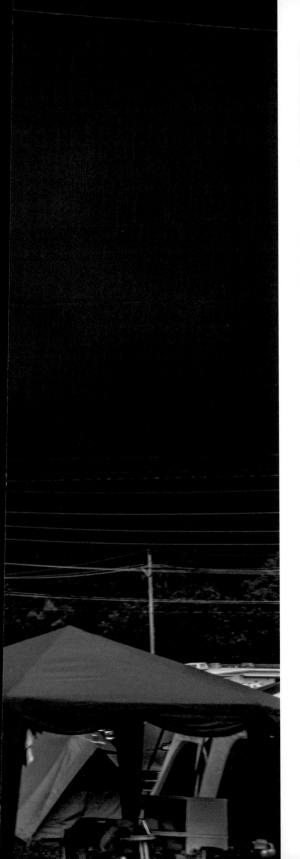

Looks like rain.

At Winfield, the rain falls on the just and the unjust, the tuned and the somewhat flat. Gore-Tex is part of the dress code. Mud's what you take back as a souvenir.

But while Mama Nature shows up for every festival in some form or other, sometimes she really outdoes herself. Floods. Tornadoes. Even an occasional September snowflake.

In 2008, Land Rushers set up camp looking like extras in the brick-making scenes of "The Ten Commandments." Still, a few soaked hours later, most of the structures were in place to give shelter from the storms.

Turned out the problem wasn't so much the rain coming down as it was the river rising up. Ten inches had fallen that Thursday night. By Monday, the Walnut was expected to crest at 34 feet — 16 feet above flood stage.

Nobody was waiting around for that. A fleet of tractors showed up with log chains, pulling everything from VW buses to cas-

tle-sized RVs out of the rising tide.

Winfield Lake turned into the destination of choice. Throughout the day, a steady stream of cars and trucks lined up for a place to camp. In sharp contrast to the demands of Land Rush, few were looking for the "perfect" place. Somewhere dry, somewhere a safe distance from the water were the only real estate criteria anyone paid attention to.

After clothes dried and water and electricity were connected, most accepted and even enjoyed the fresh perspective the move had given them. Outlying stages including Stage 5 opened for business. Newcomers, like

Flood Stage, made the best of the situation.

By the official start of the festival, the water had dropped to the point where the grandstands and other fairground facilities were usable. The ground's campsites, however, were soaked mud pits.

Buses provided by the festival made hourly pick-ups and drop-offs at the temporary sites, people still lined up for the official shows, and – all things considered – the festival carried on in fine form.

In fact, more than a few festival goers suggested WVF try the setup again sometime.

Yeah. That's not gonna happen.

69

"When we started coming to Winfield years ago, we had two tents. Now we have two refrigerators."

– *Lori Davidson*

Winfield is a great place for people-watching. In fact, Winfield's a great place for everything-watching.

Where traditions never end.

Significant Events you're likely to stumble onto as you walk through the camp groves:
• Beatles Night
• Oh Brother Where Art Thou! Drive In Movie, Stage 5
• International Rock-Paper-Scissors Championship
• Rat Camp Band Scramble
• Four-person Scramble golf tournament
• Songs You Can't Sing for Mama
• Chick Pick
• Folding Chairs Pyramid Raids
• Midnight Bacon
• Carp Camp Parade
• Blue Hands Festival
• Anything that anyone has done two years in a row and so will continue to do every year 'til the sun burns out.

If Winfield is music's one-of-a-kind festival, then Carp is its one-of-a-kind camp.

It's easy to find. Just look for the big tent in the West Campground with the flying carp windsock, filled with hammer dulcimers, mandolins, guitars, fiddles, even a banjo and an accordion or two. And music stands. Lots of music stands.

Unlike most camps where a few players call out songs for jams and solos, Carp Camp is fueled by the power of musical unison of dozens of players. Early in the year, participants receive "homework" – a thick stack of songs that will make up September's night music.

Come the festival, players of all kinds of instruments and a wide variety of musical accomplishments are welcomed in the camp.

While there's no soloing per se, Dave Firestine and other leaders keep the music fresh by calling out different sections to play. "Fiddles!" "Guitars!" "Gallagher guitars!" "White shoes!" "Lacy underwear!" And "Clean underwear," a guaranteed set silencer.

From a "The Good, The Bad, & The Ugly" themed play to "Sound of Music" dress-up night, the group's up for anything. "We don't get much of a chance to take in the grandstand shows," Firestine said. "But a lot of performers end up here. They're looking for fun. And that's what we're all about."

"Winfield is the reunion of
the family I got to choose."

This is a judgment-free zone with lots of of room for comfort. It's plenty big enough to dance like nobody's watching, to sing like you know all the words, to love and live like it's heaven on earth.

What a place to be a kid.

Watching kids just being kids at Winfield can take you back a few decades. There's plenty of room and other kids to play with and watchful village eyes here to remind you of a slower, simpler, Mayberry kind of place that maybe never really existed – but does now.

Times being what they are, you'll see plenty of computer games in use. But those gamers also know how to flip on an electronic tuner and hold their own trading licks on songs older than anyone in the camp.

Helping keep that musical tradition alive are Andy May's Acoustic Kids workshops – a non-competitive showcase that provides support and encouragement for young players at all levels. Since 1989, Acoustic Kids has helped make the festival a great place for kids to play, and to be heard.

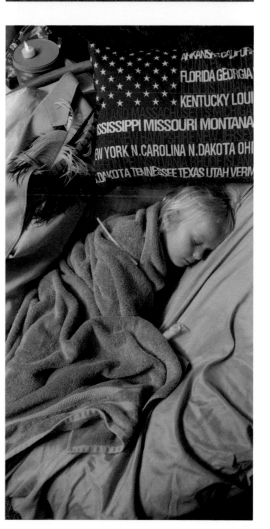

Let There Be Songs To Fill The Air.

Where two or three are gathered in Winfield, there's likely gonna be a jam.

Jamming, or jam sessions, go back further than bluegrass, to summer-night front porches where families and company shared songs. They're unplanned, unscripted, and unpredictable. More often than not, they can be the best music you'll hear all festival.

Like the participants themselves, jams at the festival come in all sorts of unique personalities. Some are small, concise circles of friends tucked between RVs. Others sprawl along with dozens of players, changing focus and style like a melodic amoeba over the course of the night.

Almost all operate with a high degree of "let's see what happens." Played out along these lines:

1: Jams often start with "Hey, how 'bout that one, oh, you know that one . . ." Through a series of subtle grunts, the group remembers the name of the song and either accepts the choice, or deposes the suggestor and settles on a Song B.

2: Songs get played in different keys, tempos, and arrangements. Occasionally, some kind soul will quickly run through the song's chords before the music starts. More often, it's every player for him or her self.

3: Usually, the jam will play at least the chorus through with no lyrics as fair warning to players who can't cut it to pack and run.

4: After the once through, someone's going to jump in with the lyrics. If it's a bluegrass tune, it'll likely involve jilted love, a .44, jailhouses and judges, and lots of "done you wrongs." If it's a gospel song, substitute a little country church and the River Jordan for the jilt and guns.

5: The jam leader will call out an instrument name, and nod to the person he or she wants to solo. For the accomplished player, this is a chance to shine, to bring together the song's nuances with the musical skills that have been woodshedded for years. For newer, more timid players, it's a fate worse than death because a 12-bar solo lasts far longer than eternity.

Calling someone to solo can be expressed by shouting, "Take it, (name of player)!" One player gracefully turned down solo opportunities by responding, "No! You take it back!"

6: The song gets played until most people have soloed, the sun's come up, or a majority of players want to mosey over to the porta potties.

7: At this point the whole process begins again. For the next 10 days.

Russell and Sherry Brace never set out to create one of Winfield's biggest musical phenomenons. All they really wanted to do was win the 1986 festival's best campsite award.

"I'd just bought a '54 Chevy wheat truck. It was the only vehicle I had, so of course I brought it to the festival," Russell said. "The people in my camp decided the bed was just about the right size for a stage, so we started building one."

With no electricity in the Pecan Grove at the time, the work took two days to do by hand. To compliment the stage's sailing ship design, Sherry hung a "Hopelessly Lost At C" banner, complete with a keyboard with two middle C's.

The hard work earned the Braces and their friends the best campsite award. But though the stage was nice to look at, there wasn't a lot of playing going on there.

"People weren't sure what to make of it," Sherry said. "It wasn't like a campfire jam area. And it sure wasn't a fairgrounds stage. To get them past their reluctance, we started offering peach cobbler and ice cream if they'd play a song or two."

The more people played there, the more lined up to take a turn. "Before long the

only way to get on stage was to get someone else off the stage," Sherry said. After the stage ship scored its second annual campsite award, the festival presented the group with a "Stage 5" sign and official WVF designation in a ceremony held on Stage 5.

By the third year, standing in line to play was replaced by a structured sign-up system. And a cord strung across 14th Street to Stage 5 made it the first place in the Pecan Grove powered by electricity.

"Around the fifth year, I realized that acts were getting a lot better," Russell said. "People started telling me they'd been practicing the whole year just so they could play our stage."

It wasn't just the amateurs who fell in love with Stage 5. Pat Flynn commented, "This place is something special." Beppe Gambetta was quoted as saying it was his "favorite place to play." Nickel Creek grew from cute to cutting edge on the stage. Split Lip Rayfield and The Wilders made their bones at Stage 5.

Over the past three decades, the Braces and their ever-growing, hard-working volunteer crew has seen and heard every kind of music Winfield has to offer, even a group of "hand farters."

"The festival has been wonderful to work with," Sherry said. "Early on, Bob Redford told us, 'This is your stage. You run it.'"

"That's what thrills me about the stages who've come after us. They're offering something Stage 5 doesn't. I love watching them grow. It reminds me of myself 30 years ago."

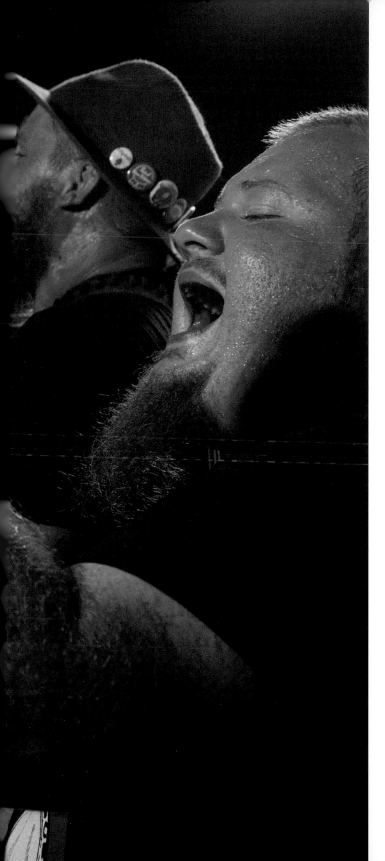

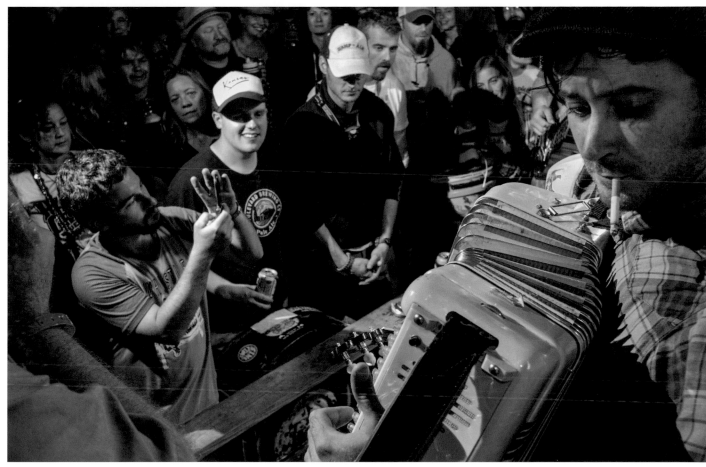

Andy Warhol gave us 15 minutes in which to be famous. Winfield gives you 10-plus days, every year. Where else can you take a stage, step up to the fire, plant yourself and your instrument in a spot in the road, and immediately find a willing, enthusiastic audience? Here, everybody is a star.
We're all "with the band."

"Every year, one tune seems to capture the spirit of the festival, becoming its own 'Orange Blossom Special,' to be heard repeatedly under the tall, Kansas walnut trees. 1982's tune, 'Sweet Georgia Brown,' was everywhere. All that was missing was the Harlem Globetrotters, passing bass runs behind their backs and balancing flatpicks on one finger."

– David McCarty

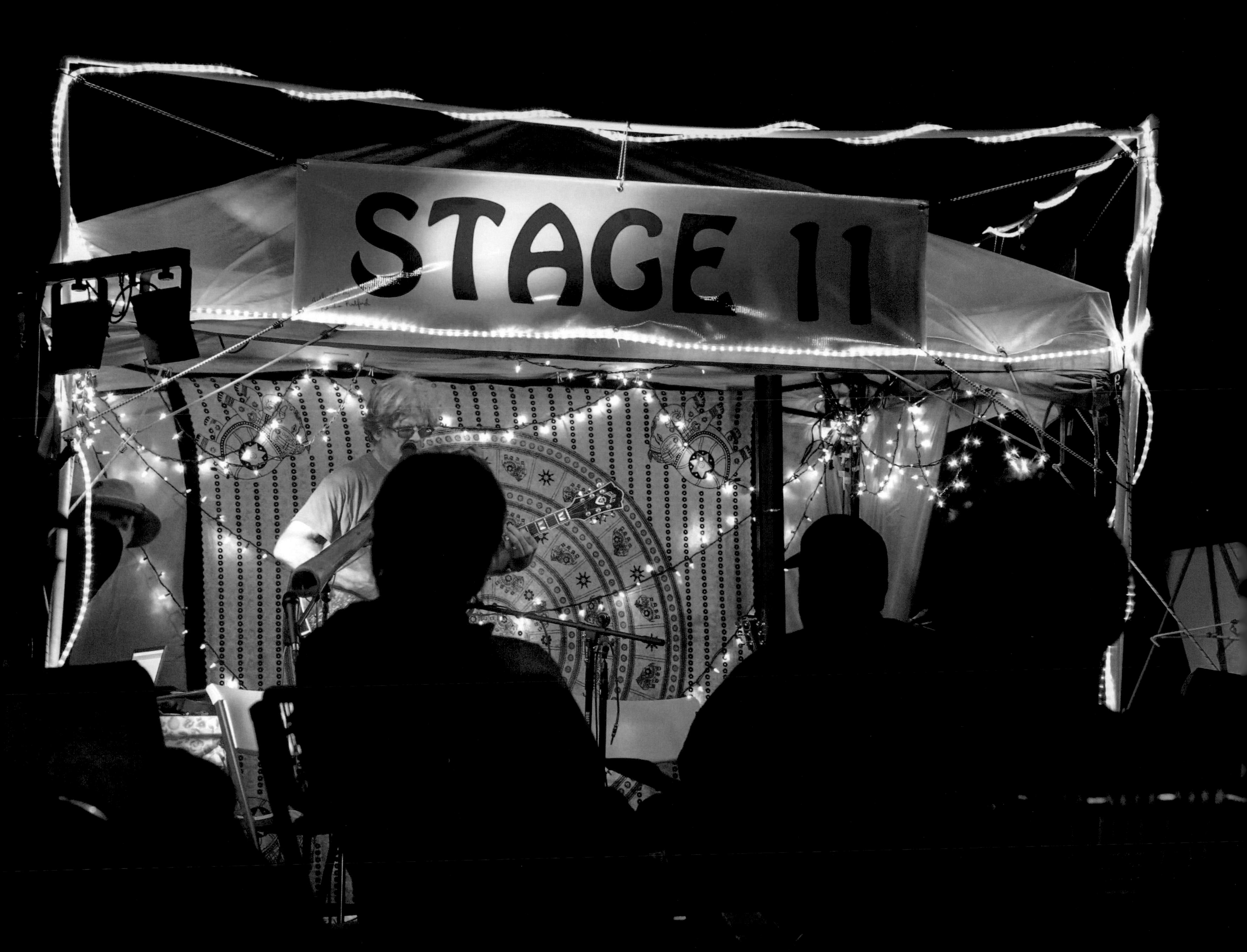
STAGE 11

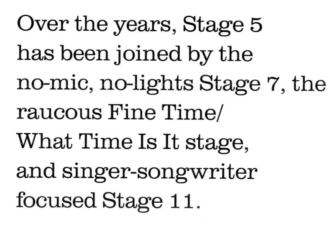

Over the years, Stage 5 has been joined by the no-mic, no-lights Stage 7, the raucous Fine Time/ What Time Is It stage, and singer-songwriter focused Stage 11.

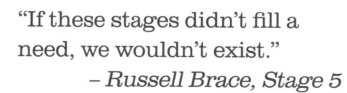

"If these stages didn't fill a need, we wouldn't exist."
– *Russell Brace, Stage 5*

"I needed to know why anyone would drive halfway across the U.S., camp in the heat, dirt, rain, cold, eat dust-filled hamburgers, just to hear four days of music that wasn't played on KEYN, mentioned by Dick Clark, or seen on MTV.

It began to dawn on me. They came to be a part of a common experience. For a while the outside world of jobs, money, problems, technology, and Ted Koppel could be held at bay. Like men of old, the magic of the campfire, the need for humanity, perhaps community, lured us out of our air-conditioned houses and offices.

Festivals like the Walnut Valley may be one of the few shared experiences we have left."

– *C.W. Page, Occasional, 1984*

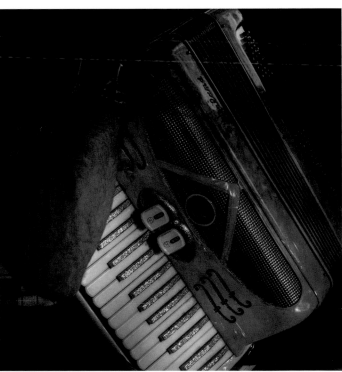

Behind every music maker at Winfield is a story that's certain to be shared:

"I traded my old sunburst Epiphone for this."

"A guy I know found it sittin' on a dusty ol' pawn shop back shelf."

"Bought it for my boy. He just might end up with it yet."

"This was Gary's guitar."

Tradition has its melancholy side, too. Empty space where people we love should be.

Things and people can't help but change from one year's snapshot to the next. Priorities shift, relationships change, obligations come due. Lives end and leave us with just faint wisps of their melodies.

Remembering what was and embracing what is in the healing arms of each other may be Winfield's greatest tradition. Maybe it's why we keep coming back with such passion.

There was supposed to be a list here, of Winfield regulars who've died in the past few years. But the project's art director, Bryan Masters, put a stop to that. There's no possible way we can include every person who ought to be listed, he said. Even if we only miss one person, that one person was an important part of someone's Winfield family. And the loss that family feels is very real.

Bryan's absolutely right. So here's to the people we've known, and to the people we never knew, but knew were loved. And here's to the new friends we'll someday meet, and forever treasure.

Norman Blake

1972

Norman Blake
Bluegrass Country Boys
Country Gazette
Dan Crary
Jim and Jesse & the Virgin-
ia Boys
Lester Flatt
New Grass Revival
Doc & Merle Watson

1973

Norman Blake
Bluegrass Country Boys
Dan Crary
J.D. Crowe and the New
South
The Lewis Family
Sue Murphy
New Grass Revival
Red, White, & Blue
Doc & Merle Watson
Clarence & Roland White

1974

Norman Blake
Bluegrass Association
Bluegrass Country Boys
Bluegrass Revue
Dan Crary
Jimmy Driftwood
Jimmy & Denzil Gyles
Ramona Jones & Friends
The Lewis Family
New Grass Revival
The Road Apples
Simmons Family
Tut Taylor
Doc & Merle Watson

1975

Cathy Barton & Dave Para
Norman Blake
Bluegrass Association
Bluegrass Country Boys
Bryan Bowers
City Limits Bluegrass Band

Dan Crary
Jimmy Driftwood
Rick George
The Gospelaires
Grand River Township
Don Lange
Dudley & Deanie Murphy
The Natural Grass
Reno, Harrell, and the
Tennessee Cutups
Larry Sparks & the Lone-
some Ramblers
Tut Taylor

1976

Byron Berline Band
Norman Blake
Bluegrass Attack
Bryan Bowers
Country Cookin'
Dan Crary
Jimmy Driftwood
Frosty Morn
John Hartford
Larry Hucke
Hutchinson Brothers
Don Lange
The Natural Grass
New Grass Revival
New Lost City Ramblers
Red, White, & Bluegrass
Smoky Valley Airlift
Sundance
Tut Taylor
Tecumseh
Thomas Singers
Town & Country Review
Happy Traum
Merle Travis
Uptown Bluegrass Band
Doc & Merle Watson
Pete Wernick
Buck White & the Down
Home Folks
Wooten Brothers

1977

Paul Adkins & Butch
Mayer
Cathy Barton & Dave Para
Norman Blake
Bluegrass Country Boys
Bryan Bowers
City Limits Bluegrass Band
Copeland Trio
Country Mile
County Line
Dan Crary
Jimmy Driftwood

Everybody & His Brother
Hickory Wind
Don Lange
Madeline MacNeil & Phil
Mason
Richard Mason
New Lost City Ramblers
Red, White, & Bluegrass
Uptown Bluegrass Band
Washboard Leo

1978

Cathy Barton & Dave Para
Norman Blake
Bryan Bowers
County Line
Dan Crary
Malcolm Dalglish & Grey
Larsen
East Creek
Cathy Fink & Duck
Donald
Lilah Gillette
Highwoods String Band
Don Lange
Madeline MacNeil & Phil
Mason
McLain Family
Dudley & Deanie Murphy
New Cache Valley Drifters
Outdoor Plumbing
Harvey Prinz & Lilah
Gillette
Red Rector & Bill Clifton
The Red Clay Ramblers
Rosy's Bar & Grill
Sparky & Rhonda Rucker
& John Davis
Art Thieme
Washboard Leo

1979

Cathy Barton & Dave Para
Ken Bloom
Bluegrass Cardinals
Bryan Bowers
Guy Carawan
Clanjamfrey
Country Ham
County Line
Dan Crary
Malcolm Dalglish & Grey
Larsen
Cathy Fink & Duck
Donald
The Folktellers
Lilah Gillette
George Gritzbach
David Holt

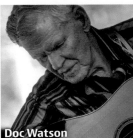
Doc Watson

Hot Rize
Bruce Hutton
Steve Kaufman
Claire Lynch & the Front
Porch String Band
Joel Mabus
Magpie
McLain Family
New Cache Valley Drifters
New Grass Revival
Lisa Null & Bill Shute
Peter Ostroushko
Harvey Prinz & Lilah
Gillette
The Red Clay Ramblers
Gamble Rogers
Sparky & Rhonda Rucker
& John Davis
Claudia Schmidt
Ed Snodderly
Talisman
Art Thieme
Ed Trickett
Jay Ungar & Lyn Hardy
Unity Bluegrass Band
Pop Wagner & Bob Bovee
Washboard Leo
Whetstone Run
Robin & Linda Williams
Wry Straw

1980

Cathy Barton & Dave Para
Norman Blake
Booger Hole Revival
Bryan Bowers
Boys in the Band
Beverly Cotten
Dan Crary
Lilah Gillette
George Gritzbach
John Hickman
Frank Hill
Hot Rize
Just Bill (Hubert)
Claire Lynch & the Front
Porch String Band

Joel Mabus
Magpie
Mid-Missouri Hell Band
Dudley & Deanie Murphy
Kevin Roth
Claudia Schmidt
Art Thieme
Doc & Merle Watson
Wry Straw

1981

Backwoods Band
Cathy Barton & Dave Para
Byron Berline Band
Norman Blake
Ken Bloom
Bluegrass Country Boys
Bryan Bowers
Beverly Cotten
Dan Crary
DeDannan
Lilah Gillette
David Grisman Quartet
Neil Hellman
John Hickman
Stanley Hicks
Hot Rize
Hotmud Family
Dan Huckabee
Kimberlite
Claire Lynch & the Front
Porch String Band
Mark Nelson
Jim Post & Randy Sabien
The Red Clay Ramblers
Mary Faith Rhoads & John
Pearse
Station Road
Art Thieme
Ron Wall
Washboard Leo

1982

Cathy Barton & Dave Para
Ken Bloom
Bryan Bowers
Company Comin'
Beverly Cotten
Country Gazette
Dan Crary
Mike Cross
DeDannan
Lilah Gillette
John Hickman
Hoofin' High Country
Cloggers
Hot Rize
Mark Kline & Mrs.
Wade Miller

Dudley & Deanie Murphy
New Grass Revival
Red & Murphy & Co.
Mary Faith Rhoads & John
Pearse
Kevin Roth
Southern Manor
Southwind
Orrin Star (with Gary
Mehalick)
Art Thieme
Undergrass Boys
Ron Wall
Doc & Merle Watson

1983

Seth Austen
Cathy Barton & Dave Para
Stevie Beck
Byron Berline Band
Becky Blackley
Ken Bloom
The Bluegrass Band
Roz Brown
Buck's Stove & Range
County Line
Dan Crary
Mike Cross
DeDannan
Foster Family String Band
Neil Hellman
John Hickman
Hoofin' High Country
Cloggers
John McCutcheon
Mark O'Connor
Chris Proctor
The Tony Rice Unit
Pat Skinner
Southern Manor
Southwind
Art Thieme
Tisra-Til
Tracy's Family Band
Trapezoid
Washboard Leo
Whetstone Run

1984

Cathy Barton & Dave Para
Stevie Beck
Byron Berline Band
Becky Blackley
Bryan Bowers
Rolly Brown
Roz Brown
Danny Carnahan & Robin
Petrie
Chameleon Puppet Theatre

Russell Cook
Patrick Couton & George
Fischer
Dan Crary
Foster Family String Band
Lindsay Haisley
John Hickman
Hot Rize
Juggernaut String
Joel Mabus
John McCutcheon
Larry McNeely
Walt Michael & Co.
New Grass Revival
Mark O'Connor
Southwind
Swiftkick Cloggers
The Tennessee Gentlemen
Art Thieme
Touchstone
Trapezoid
Tony Trischka & Skyline

1985

Cathy Barton & Dave Para
Stevie Beck
Byron Berline Band
Becky Blackley
Blue Night Express
Roz Brown
Chameleon Puppet Theatre
Cloud Valley
Russell Cook
Dan Crary
Mike Cross
Doug Dillard Band
Pat Donohue
Chris Duffy Trio
Beppe Gambetta
Green Grass Cloggers
Lindsay Haisley
John Hickman
Horse Sense
Hot Shandy
Pat Kirtley
Eric Lugosch
John McCutcheon
Nashville Bluegrass Band
Mark Nelson
New Grass Revival
The Red Clay Ramblers
Mary Faith Rhoads & John
Pearse
Gamble Rogers
Shady Grove Band
Lynn & Liz Shaw
Art Thieme
Tony Trischka & Skyline
Washboard Leo

1986
Seth Austen
Cathy Barton & Dave Para
Stevie Beck
Byron Berline Band
Becky Blackley
Bryan Bowers
Roz Brown
Chameleon Puppet Theatre
Dan Crary
Mike Cross
Dab Hand
Lindsay Haisley
John Hickman
Hoofin' High Country Cloggers
Hot Rize
Eileen Ivers
John McCutcheon
Mick Moloney, O'Connell & Keane
Mark O'Connor
Chris Proctor
Peter Rowan
The Special Consensus
Art Thieme
Aileen & Elkin Thomas
Ed Trickett
Tony Trischka & Skyline
Doc Watson & Jack Lawrence

1987
Linda Allen
Stevie Beck
Byron Berline Band
Becky Blackley
Roz Brown
Chameleon Puppet Theatre
Dan Crary
Mike Cross
Foster Family String Band
Full Circle
Good Ol' Persons
Lindsay Haisley
Neil Hellman
Tim Henderson
John Hickman
Hoofin' High Country Cloggers
Horse Sense
Hot Rize
Last Kansas Exit
John McCutcheon
Walt Michael & Co.
New Grass Revival
Harvey Reid
Hugh Sparks

Aileen & Elkin Thomas
Total Strangers
Doc Watson & Jack Lawrence
Wood's Tea Co.

1988
David Amram
Cathy Barton & Dave Para
Bluegrass Country Boys
Bluestem
Roz Brown
Chameleon Puppet Theatre
Tom Chapin & Friends
Dan Crary
Mike Cross
John Hartford
John Hickman
Hoofin' High Country Cloggers
Hot Rize
Alison Krauss & Union Station
John McCutcheon
Walt Michael & Co.
No Strings Attached
Redwing
Reel World String Band
Harvey Reid
Mike Snider
The Special Consensus
Aileen & Elkin Thomas
Doc Watson & Jack Lawrence

1989
Bell & Shore
Bennett Brothers
Byron Berline Band
BCH (Berline, Crary, Hickman), and Moore
Blue Rose (Fink, Marxer, L.Lewis)
Bluestem
Bryan Bowers
Roz Brown
Buzzard Rock String Band
Chameleon Puppet Theatre
Tom Chapin & Friends
Dan Crary
Danger in the Air
Cathy Fink & Marcy Marxer
Four Hands in a Cloud of Dust (puppets)
Full Circle
Lilah Gillette
Steve Gillette & Cindy Mangsen

John Hickman
Hoofin' High Country Cloggers
John McCutcheon
Walt Michael & Co.
New Grass Revival
Harvey Reid
Phil Salazar Band
Shady Grove Band
The Special Consensus
Spontaneous Combustion
Aileen & Elkin Thomas
Linda Tilton
Happy Traum
Turtle Creek

1990
Paul Adkins & the Borderline Band
Paul Adkins & Butch Mayer
Byron Berline Band
BCH (Berline, Crary, Hickman), and Moore
Bluestem
Roz Brown
Tom Chapin & Friends
Dan Crary
Mike Cross
Danger in the Air
Julie Davis
Judy Dees
Dixie Chicks
Cathy Fink & Marcy Marxer
Four Hands in a Cloud of Dust (puppets)
The Gallier Band
Lilah Gillette
Dana Hamilton + 2
John Hickman
Hoofin' High Country Cloggers
The House Band
Steve Kaufman
Andy May
John McCutcheon
Walt Michael & Co.
Northern Lights
Harvey Reid
Steve Smith
The Special Consensus
Spontaneous Combustion
Art Thieme
Aileen & Elkin Thomas
Linda Tilton
Trapezoid
Happy Traum
Turtle Creek

Wild Rose Ensemble

1991
Cathy Barton & Dave Para
Stephen Bennett & Bill Gurley
Norman Blake
The Bluegrass Patriots
Bryan Bowers
Roz Brown
Dan Crary
Mike Cross
Danger in the Air
Julie Davis
DeDannan
Dixie Chicks
Mike Fenton
Lilah Gillette
Hoofin' High Country Cloggers
Steve Kaufman
Alison Krauss & Union Station
Loose Ties
Claire Lynch & the Front Porch String Band
Joel Mabus
Andy May
John McCutcheon
The Lynn Morris Band
New Prairie Ramblers
The New Tradition
Mark O'Connor
David Schnaufer
The Bill Sky Family
Spontaneous Combustion
Aileen & Elkin Thomas
Linda Tilton
Happy Traum
Turtle Creek

1992
Paul Adkins & the Borderline Band
Paul Adkins & Butch Mayer
Stephen Bennett
Bluestem
Saul Brody
Roz Brown
Tom Chapin & Friends
Colcannon
Mike Cross
Dixie Chicks
Dennis Doyle
Friedlander & Hall
Front Range
Beppe Gambetta
Lilah Gillette

Byron Berline

Steve Gillette & Cindy Mangsen
Jane Gillman
Slavik Hanzlik
Steve Kaufman
Laughing Matters
Andy May
John McCutcheon
Karen Mueller
The New Tradition
No Strings Attached
Andy Owens Project
Ranch Romance
Sparky & Rhonda Rucker & John Davis
Mary Caitlin Smith
The Special Consensus
Spontaneous Combustion
Aileen & Elkin Thomas
Linda Tilton

1993
Cathy Barton & Dave Para
BCH (Berline, Crary, Hickman), and Moore
Bryan Bowers
Roz Brown
California
Dan Crary
Julie Davis
Pat Donohue
Beppe Gambetta
Paul & Win Grace and Family
John Hickman
Steve Kaufman
Peter Keane
Alison Krauss & Union Station
Laughing Matters
Loose Ties
Andy May
John McCutcheon
Karen Mueller
The New Tradition
No Strings Attached
Tim & Mollie O'Brien &

the O'Boys
Andy Owens Project
Barry Patton
Tom Paxton
Ranch Romance
Revival
Scartaglen
Mary Caitlin Smith
Spontaneous Combustion
St. James's Gate + Colm
Ivan Stiles
Sugarbeat
Linda Tilton
Mark Tindle
Robin & Linda Williams
Radim Zenkl

1994
Duck Baker & Molly Andrews
George Balderose
Bill Barwick
Stephen Bennett
Byron Berline Band
BCH (Berline, Crary, Hickman), and Moore
Bluestem
Roz Brown
California
Tom Chapin & Friends
Cooper, Nelson & Goelz
Dan Crary
Mike Cross
Julie Davis
Druhá Tráva
Cathy Fink & Marcy Marxer
Front Range
John Hickman
Crow Johnson
Makin' Memories
Marley's Ghost
Andy May
John McCutcheon
New Potatoes
The New Tradition
Nickel Creek
Nonesuch
Barry Patton
Pfeiffer Brothers
Ranch Romance
Lou Reid, Terry Baucom & Carolina
Revival
Mary Caitlin Smith
The Special Consensus
Spontaneous Combustion
St. James's Gate + Colm
Art Thieme

Aileen & Elkin Thomas
Linda Tilton
Winfield Regional Symphony
Radim Zenkl

1995
Bill Barwick
Byron Berline Band
BCH (Berline, Crary, Hickman), and Moore
Bluegrass Etc.
The Bluegrass Patriots
Bryan Bowers
Roz Brown
California
Tom Chapin & Friends
Dan Crary
Mike Cross
Julie Davis
Phyllis Dunne
Friedlander & Hall
Beppe Gambetta
John Hickman
Crow Johnson
Steve Kaufman
Marley's Ghost
Andy May
John McCutcheon
Nickel Creek
Nonesuch
Tim & Mollie O'Brien & the O'Boys
David Parmley, Scott Vestal & Continental Divide
Barry Patton
Tom Paxton
The Plaid Family
Revival
Mike Seeger
Mary Caitlin Smith
Red Steagall & the Coleman Co. Cowboys
Aileen & Elkin Thomas
Linda Tilton
Winfield City Band
The Young Acoustic Allstars

1996
Eddie Adcock Band
Charles David Alexander
Cathy Barton & Dave Para
Bill Barwick
Byron Berline Band
BCH (Berline, Crary, Hickman), and Moore
Blue Highway
Bluestem

Bryan Bowers
Roz Brown
Tom Chapin & Friends
Cherish the Ladies
Chesapeake
Dan Crary
Mike Cross
Julie Davis
Pat Donohue
Beppe Gambetta
Grass Is Greener
John Hickman
Crow Johnson
Steve Kaufman
Steven King
Pat Kirtley
Marley's Ghost
Andy May
John McCutcheon
Karen Mueller
The New Tradition
Nickel Creek
Tim & Mollie O'Brien & the O'Boys
Mark O'Connor
Barry Patton
Tom Paxton
The Plaid Family
Revival
David Schnaufer
Mary Caitlin Smith
Spontaneous Combustion
Ivan Stiles
Aileen & Elkin Thomas
Linda Tilton
Winfield Regional Symphony

1997
Eddie Adcock Band
Cathy Barton & Dave Para
Bill Barwick
Stephen Bennett & Bill Gurley
Byron Berline Band
Black Rose
Bluestem
Roz Brown
Tom Chapin & Friends
Cherish the Ladies
Jon Cobert
Dan Crary
Julie Davis
Judith Edelman Band
The Freight Hoppers
Front Range
Beppe Gambetta
Dana Hamilton + 2
Crow Johnson

Steve Kaufman
Marley's Ghost
Andy May
John McCutcheon
The New Tradition
Nickel Creek
No Strings Attached
Barry Patton
Tom Paxton
Chris Proctor
Revival
Small Potatoes
Mary Caitlin Smith
Spontaneous Combustion
Aileen & Elkin Thomas
Linda Tilton
Ron Wall
Eric Weissberg

1998
Cathy Barton & Dave Para
Bill Barwick
Stephen Bennett
Bluestem
Bryan Bowers
Roz Brown
Tom Chapin & Friends
Cherish the Ladies
Dan Crary
Mike Cross
Crucial Smith
Julie Davis
Bob Franke
Beppe Gambetta
Steve Gillette & Cindy Mangsen
Paul Goelz
Hickory Hill
Home Rangers
Leon Howell
Crow Johnson
Steve Kaufman
Laurie Lewis
Live Bait
Claire Lynch & the Front Porch String Band
Marley's Ghost
Andy May
John McCutcheon
Karen Mueller
The New Tradition
New West
No Strings Attached
Barry Patton
The Plaid Family
Small Potatoes
Spontaneous Combustion
Still on the Hill
Aileen & Elkin Thomas

Linda Tilton
Toucan Jam
Wild & Blue

1999
Bill Barwick
Byron Berline Band
Blue Plate Special
The Bluegrass Pals
Roz Brown
Crucial Smith
Julie Davis
Pat Donohue
Connie Dover, Roger Landes & Friends
The Euphoria Stringband
Nick Forster & Friends
The Freight Hoppers
Beppe Gambetta
Adie Grey & Dave MacKenzie
Grubstake
Harmonious Wail
Crow Johnson
Steve Kaufman
Pat Kirtley
Dan Levenson
Marley's Ghost
Andy May
John McCutcheon
Tim O'Brien & Darrell Scott
Pagosa Hot Strings
Barry Patton
Prickly Pear & the Cactus Chorale
The Renters
Ruby's Begonia
Safe Harbor
David Schnaufer & Stephen Seifert
Serenata
Small Potatoes
The Special Consensus
Spontaneous Combustion
Ivan Stiles
Still on the Hill
Aileen & Elkin Thomas
Linda Tilton
Toucan Jam
Pete Wernick's Live Five/Flexigrass

2000
Bar-D Wranglers
Cathy Barton & Dave Para
Bill Barwick
Stephen Bennett
Byron Berline Band

Big Twang
Bluestem
Bryan Bowers
Roz Brown
Michael Chapdelaine
Tom Chapin & Friends
Cherish the Ladies
Dan Crary
Dan Crary, Lonnie Hoppers, and their American Band
Mike Cross
Crucial Smith
Tommy Emmanuel
Beppe Gambetta
Los Harmonica Hombres y una Mujer
Home Rangers
Jana Jae & Friends
Crow Johnson
Steve Kaufman
Pat Kirtley
The Krüger Brothers
Dan Levenson
Marley's Ghost
Andy May
John McCutcheon
Misty River
Karen Mueller
Nickel Creek
No Strings Attached
Barry Patton
The Plaid Family
Prickly Pear & the Cactus Chorale
Revival
David Schnaufer & Stephen Seifert
Small Potatoes
Spontaneous Combustion
Aileen & Elkin Thomas
Linda Tilton
The Wilders

2001
Cathy Barton & Dave Para
Bill Barwick
Stephen Bennett
Byron Berline Band
Big Twang
Bluestem
Roz Brown
Michael Chapdelaine
Tom Chapin & Friends
Dan Crary
Julie Davis
Don Edwards
Exit 81
Fragment

The Gallier Brothers
Beppe Gambetta
Hickory Project
Jim Hurst & Missy Raines
Pete Huttlinger with Mollie Weaver
Kansas Heart
Pat Kirtley
Dan Levenson
Andy May
John McCutcheon
Misty River
Pagosa Hot Strings
Barry Patton
Prairie Rose Wranglers
Mark Schatz & Friends
Shenanigans
Small Potatoes
Sons of the San Joaquin
Spontaneous Combustion
Aileen & Elkin Thomas
Linda Tilton
Kelly and Diana Werts
The Wilders

2002
Bill Barwick
Stephen Bennett
Bluestem
Roz Brown
Tom Chapin & Friends
Mike Cross
Crucial Smith
Dakota Blonde
Julie Davis
Pat Donohue
Don Edwards
Tommy Emmanuel
Exit 81
Robert Force
The Gallier Brothers
Beppe Gambetta
Henri's Notions
Hot Club of Cowtown
Jim Hurst & Missy Raines
Pete Huttlinger with Mollie Weaver
Crow Johnson
Pat Kirtley
Laurie Lewis
David Mallett
Marley's Ghost
Andy May
John McCutcheon
Misty River
Karen Mueller
No Strings Attached
Barry Patton
Prairie Rose Wranglers

Beppe Gambetta

Red Wine
Sons of the San Joaquin
Spontaneous Combustion
Linda Tilton
Walnut Valley Men's Chorus
The Wilders
Brooks Williams

2003
Bill Barwick
Stephen Bennett
Roz Brown
Nick Charles
Dan Crary
Julie Davis
Daybreak
Tommy Emmanuel
Pat Flynn, John Cowan & Friends with special guest Stuart Duncan
Heartstrings
Hickory Project
Hot Club of Cowtown
Pete Huttlinger with Mollie Weaver
Crow Johnson
Mark Johnson & Emory Lester
Marley's Ghost
Andy May
John McCutcheon
Modern Hicks
Karen Mueller
Kacey Musgraves
No Strings Attached
Barry Patton
Prairie Rose Wranglers
Prickly Pear & the Cactus Chorale
John Reischman and the Jaybirds
Small Potatoes
The Special Consensus
Spontaneous Combustion
Linda Tilton
Walnut River String Band

Walnut Valley Men's Chorus
Barry Ward
The Wilders
Yonder Mountain String Band

2004
Bill Barwick
Stephen Bennett
Byron Berline Band
Bluestem
Roz Brown
Tom Chapin & Friends
Nick Charles
Cherish the Ladies
Dan Crary
Mike Cross
Julie Davis
Doyle Dykes
Tommy Emmanuel
Pat Flynn, John Cowan, Stuart Duncan & Scott Vestal
The Gallier Brothers
Beppe Gambetta
Les Gustafson-Zook
Hot Club of Cowtown
Kane's River
Marley's Ghost
Andy May
John McCutcheon
Men of Steel
Barry Patton
John Reischman and the Jaybirds
Small Potatoes
Spontaneous Combustion
Alan Thornhill
Linda Tilton
Harry Tuft
Kendra Ward & Bob Bence
The Waybacks
Pete Wernick's Live Five/Flexigrass
The Wilders

2005
Bill Barwick
Stephen Bennett
Byron Berline Band
Roz Brown
Tom Chapin & Friends
The John Cowan Band
Julie Davis
Tommy Emmanuel
Steve Eulberg
Bob Evans
Pat Flynn & Friends

The Greencards
Adie Grey & Dave MacKenzie
Pete Huttlinger with Mollie Weaver
Chris Jones & the Night Drivers
King Wilkie
Marley's Ghost
Andy May
Tim May & Plaid Grass
John McCutcheon
David Munnelly Band
No Strings Attached
Barry Patton
Sons of the San Joaquin
Spontaneous Combustion
Still on the Hill
Tennessee HeartStrings Band
Linda Tilton
The Waybacks
The Wilders
Williams & Clark Expedition

2006
Cathy Barton & Dave Para
Bill Barwick
Stephen Bennett
Byron Berline Band
Bluestem
Roz Brown
Cadillac Sky
Tom Chapin & Friends
Nick Charles
Dan Crary & Thunderation
Julie Davis
Tommy Emmanuel
Pat Flynn, Buddy Greene & Friends
Bruce Graybill
The Greencards
Brian Henke
Hot Strings
Pete Huttlinger with Mollie Weaver
Chris Jones & the Night Drivers
Steve Kaufman
Dan LaVoie
Marley's Ghost
Andy May
John McCutcheon
Andy McKee
Misty River
Mountain Smoke
David Munnelly Band
Tim O'Brien Trio

Barry Patton
Small Potatoes
Jo Ann Smith & Pocket Change
Spontaneous Combustion
Dave Stamey
Still on the Hill
Linda Tilton
The Waybacks
The Wilders
Adrienne Young & Little Sadie

2007
Bill Barwick
Bluestem
Ronnie Bowman & The Committee
Roz Brown
Cadillac Sky
Brad Davis, Tim May & John Moore
Julie Davis
Tommy Emmanuel
Pat Flynn
Beppe Gambetta
The Greencards
Greenwillis
Adie Grey & Dave MacKenzie
Michael Reno Harrell
Brian Henke
Pete Huttlinger with Mollie Weaver
Kansas Heart
Marley's Ghost
Andy May
John McCutcheon
Mountain Smoke
David Munnelly Band
Alecia Nugent
The Old 78s
Barry Patton
Kenny & Amanda Smith
Dave Stamey
Still on the Hill
Linda Tilton
The Wilders
The Wiyos
Wood's Tea Co.

2008
Bill Barwick
Stephen Bennett
Byron Berline Band
Roz Brown
Tom Chapin & Friends
Dailey & Vincent
Julie Davis

Diamond W Wranglers
Beppe Gambetta
The Greencards
Buddy Greene, Ron Block & Jeff Taylor
Michael Reno Harrell
Pete Huttlinger with Mollie Weaver
Chris Jones & the Night Drivers
The Randy Kohrs Band
Marley's Ghost
Andy May
John McCutcheon
Adam Miller
Misty River
Mountain Heart
David Munnelly Band
The Old 78s
Barry Patton
Rockin' Acoustic Circus
Small Potatoes
Doug Smith
Kenny & Amanda Smith
Johnny Staats & Robert Shafer
Dave Stamey
Still on the Hill
Thomas/Delancey Trio
Linda Tilton
The Wiyos

2009
Bill Barwick
Stephen Bennett
Roz Brown
Tom Chapin & Friends
Julie Davis
Beppe Gambetta
The Greencards
Buddy Greene, Ron Block & Jeff Taylor
Pete Huttlinger with Mollie Weaver
The Infamous Stringdusters
Wil Maring & Robert Bowlin
Marley's Ghost
Andy May
John McCutcheon
Adam Miller
David Moran, Joe Morgan & Friends
Mountain Heart
Mountain Smoke
David Munnelly Band
Notorious Folk
Barry Patton
Kati Penn & NewTown

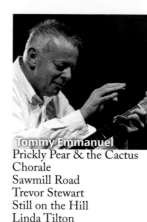
Tommy Emmanuel

Prickly Pear & the Cactus Chorale
Sawmill Road
Trevor Stewart
Still on the Hill
Linda Tilton
The Wilders
The Wiyos

2010
Bill Barwick
Roz Brown
The Chapmans
Nick Charles
Dan Crary
Julie Davis
The Farewell Drifters
The Greencards
Hickory Project
The Hillbenders
Houston Jones
Sierra Hull & Highway 111
Pat Kirtley
The Randy Kohrs Band
Andy May
John McCutcheon
MilkDrive
Mountain Heart
Mountain Smoke
No Strings Attached
Notorious Folk
Barry Patton
Prickly Pear & the Cactus Chorale
Kevin Roth
Small Potatoes
Trevor Stewart
Still on the Hill
Téada
Linda Tilton
Barry Ward
The Wilders
Josh Williams Band
The Wiyos

2011
Cathy Barton & Dave Para
Bill Barwick

Stephen Bennett
Byron Berline Band
Bettman & Halpin
Bluestem
Bryan Bowers
Roz Brown
Tom Chapin & Friends
Dan Crary & Thunderation
Mike Cross
Julie Davis
Tommy Emmanuel
The Gallier Band
Beppe Gambetta
Hot Club of Cowtown
Pete Huttlinger with Mollie Weaver
Eileen Ivers & Immigrant Soul
Pat Kirtley
Marley's Ghost
Andy May
John McCutcheon
Michael Martin Murphey with special guest Pat Flynn
Notorious Folk
Barry Patton
Prairie Fire
Prairie Rose Rangers
Revival
Kenny & Amanda Smith
Trevor Stewart
Still on the Hill
Tanaka Akihiro
Linda Tilton
Mark Alan Wade Trio
Barry Ward
The Wilders

2012
Bill Barwick
Stephen Bennett
Roz Brown
Dan Crary & Thunderation
Julie Davis
Driven
Steve Eulberg
The Greencards
Michael Reno Harrell Trio
Jim Hurst
Claire Lynch Band
Marley's Ghost
Andy May
John McCutcheon
Mountain Heart
NewFound Road
Notorious Folk
Barry Patton
The Quebe Sisters Band
Revival

Jo Ann Smith & Friends
Richard Smith and Julie Adams
The Steel Wheels
Still on the Hill
Téada
3 Trails West
Linda Tilton
Mark Alan Wade Trio
Barry Ward

2013
Bill Barwick
Stephen Bennett
Byron Berline Band
Roz Brown
Tom Chapin & Friends
Driven
Beppe Gambetta
The Grascals
Buddy Greene, Ron Block & Sierra Hull
The Haunted Windchimes
Pete Huttlinger with Mollie Weaver
Marley's Ghost
Andy May
John McCutcheon
MilkDrive
Adam Miller
Mischievous Swing
David Munnelly Duo
Barry Patton
The Prowell Family
Scenic Roots
Steve & Ruth Smith
The Special Consensus
Dave Stamey
The Steel Wheels
Still on the Hill
Tim & Myles Thompson
Linda Tilton
ToneBlazers
Winfield City Band

2014
Bill Barwick
Bettman & Halpin
Bluestem
The Boxcars
Roz Brown
Cherokee Maidens & Sycamore Swing
Detour
Driven
FiddleWhamdiddle
The Greencards
Pete Huttlinger with Mollie Weaver

Jacob Johnson
Kane's River
Andy May
Tim May & Steve Smith
John McCutcheon
Mischievous Swing
Mountain Smoke
Barry Patton
The Rambling Rooks
Revival
Allen Shadd, Jack Lawrence, & T. Michael Coleman
Small Potatoes
Kenny & Amanda Smith
Socks in the Frying Pan
Dave Stamey
The Steel Wheels
Still on the Hill
Tim & Myles Thompson
Linda Tilton

2015
Stephen Bennett
Byron Berline Band
Roz Brown
Tom Chapin & Friends
Cherokee Maidens & Sycamore Swing
Dan Crary, Bill Evans & Steve Spurgin
Della Mae
Detour
Driven
Michael Reno Harrell Trio
Pete Huttlinger with Mollie Weaver
Jacob Johnson
Marley's Ghost
Andy May
John McCutcheon
Notorious Folk
The O'Connor Family Band
The Paperboys
Barry Patton
Prairie Rose Rangers
The Roys
Scenic Roots
Jo Ann Smith & Friends
Socks in the Frying Pan
The Steel Wheels
Still on the Hill
The Tannahill Weavers
Theory Expats
Linda Tilton
Barry Ward

Peter Ostroushko

1972

National Flat Pick Guitar Championship
1. Jimmy Gyles
2. Jeffrey Pearson
3. Jim Ruth

1973

National Flat Pick Guitar Championship
1. Jimmy Gyles
2. Dudley Murphy
3. Robert Abrams

Walnut Valley Old Time Fiddle Championship
1. Jeff Pritchard
2. John Sommers
3. Bill Reser

1974

National Flat Pick Guitar Championship
1. Rick George
2. Mark O'Connor
3. Peter shko

National Bluegrass Banjo Championship
1. Lynn Morris
2. Randy Alexander
3. Jeff Kimbal

Walnut Valley Old Time Fiddle Championship
1. Mark O'Connor
2. Jeff Pritchard
3. David Coe

1975

National Flat Pick Guitar Championship
1. Mark O'Connor
2. Chris Phillips
3. Greg Henkle

National Bluegrass Banjo Championship
1. Randal Morton
2. Dwight Williams
3. Richie Mintz

Walnut Valley Old Time Fiddle Championship
1. Jeff Pritchard
2. Henry the Fiddler
3. Gary Wackerly

1976

National Flat Pick Guitar Championship
1. Orrin Star
2. Billy Kay
3. Jimmy Gyles

National Bluegrass Banjo Championship
1. Mark Maniscalo
2. Steve Hanson
3. Gary Gray

National Mountain Dulcimer Championship
1. David Schnaufer
2. Richard Coe
3. Jim French

Walnut Valley Old Time Fiddle Championship
1. Dick Barrett
2. Mark O'Connor
3. Jeff Pritchard

Walnut Valley Mandolin Championship (1976-2009)
1. Jimmy Gyles
2. Orrin Star
3. Mark O'Connor

1977

National Flat Pick Guitar Championship
1. Mark O'Connor
2. Steve Kaufman
3. Billy Kay

National Bluegrass Banjo Championship
1. Steve Hanson
2. Gary Gray
3. Bill Perry, Jr.

National Hammer Dulcimer Championship
1. Bob Wey

Mark O'Connor

2. Mary F. Rhoads
3. Don Gillett

National Mountain Dulcimer Championship
1. Chris Patterson
2. Richard Coe
3. Bonnie Carol

Walnut Valley Old Time Fiddle Championship
1. Mark nor
2. Jeff Pritchard
3. Russell O'Neal

Walnut Valley Mandolin Championship (1976-2009)
1. Clyde Moon
2. Craig Fletcher
3. Craig Willoughby

1978

National Flat Pick Guitar Championship
1. Steve Kaufman
2. Robert Bowlin
3. Chris Biggs

National Bluegrass Banjo Championship
1. Danny Gilliland
2. Steven Block
3. Allan Walton

National Hammer Dulcimer Championship
1. Sam Herrmann
2. Greg Becker
3. Kim Becker

National Mountain Dulcimer Championship
1. Randy Wilkinson
2. Bonnie Carol
3. Rodger Harris

Walnut Valley Old Time Fiddle Championship

1. Murray Willoughby
2. Joe Cotton
3. Ted Smith

Walnut Valley Mandolin Championship (1976-2009)
1. Dana Mohr
2. Craig Willoughby
3. Ted Smith

1979

National Flat Pick Guitar Championship
1. Roger Ferguson
2. Steve Hanson
3. Chris Biggs

National Bluegrass Banjo Championship
1. Gary "Biscuit" Davis
2. Scott Vestal
3. David Bennett

National Hammer Dulcimer Championship
1. Bruce Warren
2. Al Jacobs
3. Linda Borcherding

National Mountain Dulcimer Championship
1. Mark Nelson
2. Larkin Bryant
3. Tom Haver

Walnut Valley Old Time Fiddle Championship
1. Johnny Murdock
2. Fred Carpenter
3. David Harvey

National Finger Style Guitar Championship (1979-2003)
1. Robert Bowlin
2. Royce Campbell
3. John Barger

Walnut Valley Mandolin Championship (1976-2009)
1. Bob Clark
2. David Harvey
3. David McCarty

1980

National Flat Pick Guitar Championship
1. Roy Curry

2. David Grier
3. Chris Biggs

National Bluegrass Banjo Championship
1. Rick Bentley
2. Billy McKinley
3. John Ramsey

National Hammer Dulcimer Championship
1. Dana Hamilton
2. Matthew Kirby
3. John Corbin Goldsberry

National Mountain Dulcimer Championship
1. Wade Hampton Miller
2. Rodger Harris
3. Jim Fyhrie

Walnut Valley Old Time Fiddle Championship
1. Wanda Vick
2. David Harvey
3. Monte Gaylord

National Finger Style Guitar Championship (1979-2003)
1. Rolly Brown
2. Danny Gotham
3. Dwight Linkhart

Walnut Valley Mandolin Championship (1976-2009)
1. David Harvey
2. Don Anderson
3. Jonathan Mann

1981

National Flat Pick Guitar Championship
1. Richard Gulley
2. Don Shelton
3. Jim Renz

International Autoharp Championship
1. Martin Schuman
2. Bonnie Phipps
3. Ron Penix

National Bluegrass Banjo Championship
1. Lynn Morris
2. Dennis Bailey
3. James McKinney

National Hammer Dulcimer Championship

1. Russell Cook
2. Lucille Reilly
3. Nick Krukovsky

National Mountain Dulcimer Championship
1. Jim Fyhrie
2. Willie Jaeger
3. Seth Austen

Walnut Valley Old Time Fiddle Championship
1. Steve Gillian
2. Edward Baggott
3. Monte Gaylord

National Finger Style Guitar Championship (1979-2003)
1. Harvey Reid
2. Seth Austen
3. Carl Jones

Walnut Valley Mandolin Championship (1976-2009)
1. Dan Harlow
2. Joey McKenzie
3. Seth Austen

1982

National Flat Pick Guitar Championship
1. Mitch Corbin
2. Robin Kessinger
3. John Borcherding

International Autoharp Championship
1. Bonnie Phipps
2. Harvey Reid
3. Dan Wiethop

National Bluegrass Banjo Championship
1. James McKinney
2. Adam Fudge
3. Dave Macon

National Hammer Dulcimer Championship
1. David Moran
2. Bonnie Carol
3. Randy Zombola

National Mountain Dulcimer Championship
1. Tom Haver
2. Bonnie Carol
3. Gib Sosman

Walnut Valley Old Time

Fiddle Championship
1. Mark Ralph
2. Jeff Pritchard
3. Bill Ward

National Finger Style Guitar Championship (1979-2003)
1. Chris Proctor
2. Pat Donohue
3. Ed Gerhard

Walnut Valley Mandolin Championship (1976-2009)
1. Mitch Corbin
2. Dave Peters
3. Joey McKenzie

1983

National Flat Pick Guitar Championship
1. Robert Shafer
2. Stephen Bennett
3. Al Smith

International Autoharp Championship
1. Jewel Boesel
2. Will Smith
3. Doug Dubois

National Bluegrass Banjo Championship
1. Mike Snider
2. Roger Matthews
3. Adam Fudge

National Hammer Dulcimer Championship
1. Doug Berch
2. Steve Smith
3. Nick Harris

National Mountain Dulcimer Championship
1. Doug Berch
2. Gary Gallier
3. Mark Biggs

Walnut Valley Old Time Fiddle Championship
1. Jeff Pritchard
2. Jimmy Gyles
3. Joey McKenzie

National Finger Style Guitar Championship (1979-2003)
1. Pat Donohue
2. Julian McKea

Alison Krauss

3. Eric Lugosch

Walnut Valley Mandolin Championship (1976-2009)
1. Dave Peters
2. Joey McKenzie
3. Bob Westfall

1984

National Flat Pick Guitar Championship
1. Steve Kaufman
2. John McGann
3. Fred Duggin

International Autoharp Championship
1. Drew Smith
2. Billy Garrison
3. Tom Schroeder

National Bluegrass Banjo Championship
1. Chris Leske
2. Adam Fudge
3. Michael Allen

National Hammer Dulcimer Championship
1. Steve Smith
2. Joseph Venegoni
3. Ben Ziaie

National Mountain Dulcimer Championship
1. Mark Biggs
2. Gary Gallier
3. Mark Tindle

Walnut Valley Old Time Fiddle Championship
1. Alison Krauss
2. Randy Howard
3. Andrea Zonn

National Finger Style Guitar Championship (1979-2003)

1. Eric Lugosch
2. Geoff Bartley
3. Bill Mize

Walnut Valley Mandolin Championship (1976-2009)
1. Paul Kramer
2. John McGann
3. Robert Shafer

1985

National Flat Pick Guitar Championship
1. Robin Kessinger
2. Ron Block
3. Bobby Trapp

International Autoharp Championship
1. Tom Schroeder
2. Billy Garrison
3. Karen Mueller

National Bluegrass Banjo Championship
1. Yoshihiro Arita
2. Adam Fudge
3. Michael Allen

National Hammer Dulcimer Championship
1. Dan Duggan
2. Randy Zombola
3. Ernie Von Feldt

National Mountain Dulcimer Championship
1. Steve Smith
2. Gary Gallier
3. Bill Hodges

Walnut Valley Old Time Fiddle Championship
1. Randy Howard
2. Betty Vornbrock
3. Marty Kaufman

National Finger Style Guitar Championship (1979-2003)
1. Bill Mize
2. Geoff Bartley
3. Stephen Bennett

Walnut Valley Mandolin Championship (1976-2009)
1. John McGann
2. Charlie Provenza
3. Randy Howard

1986

National Flat Pick Guitar Championship
1. Steve Kaufman
2. Peter McLaughlin
3. Bob Minner, Jr.

International Autoharp Championship
1. Karen Mueller
2. Drew Smith
3. Tom Schroeder

National Bluegrass Banjo Championship
1. Michael Allen
2. Gary "Biscuit" Davis
3. Gerald Jones

National Hammer Dulcimer Championship
1. David James
2. Randy Barnes
3. Ernie Von Feldt

National Mountain Dulcimer Championship
1. Mark Tindle
2. Steve Smith
3. Bill Hodges

Walnut Valley Old Time Fiddle Championship
1. Jeff Guernsey
2. Randy Howard
3. Alison

National Finger Style Guitar Championship (1979-2003)
1. Phil Heywood
2. Geoff Bartley
3. Eric Lugosch

Walnut Valley Mandolin Championship (1976-2009)
1. Raymond Legere
2. Paul Glasse
3. Charlie Provenza

1987

National Flat Pick Guitar Championship
1. Stephen Bennett
2. Gary Bell
3. Bob Minner, Jr.

International Autoharp Championship
1. Mike Fenton

Stephen Bennett

2. Margie Earles
3. Ivan Stiles

National Bluegrass Banjo Championship
1. Tony Furtado
2. John Wheat
3. Mike Bub

National Hammer Dulcimer Championship
1. Dave Neiman
2. Randy Zombola
3. Andrea Lynn Ford

National Mountain Dulcimer Championship
1. Gary Gallier
2. Gib Sosman
3. Dana Hamilton

Walnut Valley Old Time Fiddle Championship
1. Bill Ward
2. Martie Erwin
3. Jeff Pritchard

National Finger Style Guitar Championship (1979-2003)
Joe Miller
1. Geoff Bartley
2. Don Ross

Walnut Valley Mandolin Championship (1976-2009)
1. Dave Peters
2. Butch Baldassari
3. Shannon Cuts

1988

National Flat Pick Guitar Championship
1. Peter McLaughlin
2. Kelly Lancaster
3. Dave Peters

International Autoharp

Championship
1. Mark Fackeldey
2. Drew Smith
3. Fredona Currie

National Bluegrass Banjo Championship
1. Gary "Biscuit" Davis
2. Mike Bub
3. Jeff Scroggins

National Hammer Dulcimer Championship
1. Randy Zombola
2. Jim Hudson
3. Dana Hamilton

National Mountain Dulcimer Championship
1. Tom Haver
2. Kim Rubert
3. Les Gallier

Walnut Valley Old Time Fiddle Championship
1. Andrea Zonn
2. Jenni Lynne Collier
3. Adam Cutts

National Finger Style Guitar Championship (1979-2003)
1. Don Ross
2. Ronald Brooks
3. Ed Hall

Walnut Valley Mandolin Championship (1976-2009)
1. Paul Glasse
2. Ben Winship
3. Matt Flinner

1989

National Flat Pick Guitar Championship
1. Gary Cook
2. Rick George
3. Rex Flinner

International Autoharp Championship
1. Stephen Young
2. Ivan Stiles
3. Les Gustafson-Zook

National Bluegrass Banjo Championship
1. Jeff Scroggins
2. Matt Flinner
3. Ted Wells

National Hammer Dulcimer Championship
1. Dana Hamilton
2. Princess Harris
3. Carey Dubbert

National Mountain Dulcimer Championship
1. Gib Sosman
2. Neil Gaston
3. Tim Simek

Walnut Valley Old Time Fiddle Championship
1. Monte Gaylord
2. Gretchen Van Houten
3. Martie Erwin

National Finger Style Guitar Championship (1979-2003)
1. Muriel Anderson
2. Ronald Brooks
3. Bradley Jones

Walnut Valley Mandolin Championship (1976-2009)
1. Paul Glasse
2. Ben Winship
3. Matt Flinner

1990

National Flat Pick Guitar Championship
1. Randy Rogers
2. Joe Payne
3. Ricky Mullins

International Autoharp Championship
1. Bill Bryant
2. Tom Schroeder
3. Ivan Stiles

National Bluegrass Banjo Championship
1. Matt Flinner
2. Jody Dennis
3. Eric Welty

National Hammer Dulcimer Championship
1. Bonnie Carol
2. Princess Harris
3. Randy Barnes

National Mountain Dulcimer Championship
1. Les Gallier
2. Mark Tindle

3. Neil Gaston

Walnut Valley Old Time Fiddle Championship
1. Randy Howard
2. Ed Carnes
3. Jason Shaw

National Finger Style Guitar Championship (1979-2003)
1. Bradley Jones
2. Ronald Brooks
3. Kelly Werts

Walnut Valley Mandolin Championship (1976-2009)
1. Randy Howard
2. Kelly Lancaster
3. Radim Zenkl

1991

National Flat Pick Guitar Championship
1. Roy Curry
2. Robert Shafer
3. Larry Lintner

International Autoharp Championship
1. Ivan Stiles
2. Les Gustafson-Zook
3. Alan Mager

National Bluegrass Banjo Championship
1. Tony Furtado
2. Steve Bush
3. Eric Welty

National Hammer Dulcimer Championship
1. Princess Harris
2. Lucille Reilly
3. Randy Barnes

National Mountain Dulcimer Championship
1. Mark Tindle
2. Neil Gaston
3. Scott Odena

Walnut Valley Old Time Fiddle Championship
1. Jason Shaw
2. Ed Carnes
3. Paul T. Brown

National Finger Style Guitar Championship (1979-2003)

1. Ed Hall
2. Edgar Cruz
3. Joe Miller

Walnut Valley Mandolin Championship (1976-2009)
1. Matt Flinner
2. Justin Bertoldie
3. Kelly Lancaster

1992

National Flat Pick Guitar Championship
1. John Shaw
2. Matt Lindsey
3. Kenny Smith

International Autoharp Championship
1. Tom Schroeder
2. Alan Mager
3. Les Gustafson-Zook

National Bluegrass Banjo Championship
1. Ira Gitlin
2. Gerald Jones
3. Sonny Smith

National Hammer Dulcimer Championship
1. Carey Dubbert
2. Greg Latta
3. Kim Murley

National Mountain Dulcimer Championship
1. Scott Odena
2. Dana Hamilton
3. Rob Brereton

Walnut Valley Old Time Fiddle Championship
1. Gretchen Van Houten
2. Ed Carnes
3. Lida Bringe

National Finger Style Guitar Championship (1979-2003)
1. Charles David Alexander
2. Eric Lugosch
3. Kelly Werts

Walnut Valley Mandolin Championship (1976-2009)
1. Radim Zenkl
2. Justin Bertoldie
3. Katsuyuki Miyazaki

1993

National Flat Pick Guitar Championship
1. Jason Shaw
2. Kenny Smith
3. Fred Duggin

International Autoharp Championship
1. Alan Mager
2. Tina Louise Barr
3. Alex Usher

National Bluegrass Banjo Championship
1. Eric Welty
2. Sonia Shell
3. Carl Anderton

National Hammer Dulcimer Championship
1. Judy Schmidt
2. Glenn McClure
3. Dean Lippincott

National Mountain Dulcimer Championship
1. Tim Simek
2. Andy Anderson
3. Evan O'Bannon

Walnut Valley Old Time Fiddle Championship
1. Ed Carnes
2. Levi Dennis
3. Monte Gaylord

National Finger Style Guitar Championship (1979-2003)
1. Tim Sparks
2. Mark Anthony Cruz
3. Marvin McDonald

Walnut Valley Mandolin Championship (1976-2009)
1. Chris Thile
2. Gary Cook
3. Scott Pearson

1994

National Flat Pick Guitar Championship
1. Mike Whitehead
2. Mark Cosgrove
3. Kenny Smith

International Autoharp Championship
1. Ron Wall

Chris Thile

2. Mike Herr
3. Lucille Reilly

National Bluegrass Banjo Championship
1. Jonathan Jones
2. Barry Palmer
3. Ray Hesson

National Hammer Dulcimer Championship
1. Renée Lippincott
2. Greg Latta
3. John Lionarons

National Mountain Dulcimer Championship
1. Alfonse Ponticelli
2. Andy Anderson
3. Robert Pearcy

Walnut Valley Old Time Fiddle Championship
1. Richard Helsley, Jr.
2. Cortland Ingram
3. John Nyen

National Finger Style Guitar Championship (1979-2003)
1. Steven King
2. Marvin McDonald
3. Pat Kirtley

Walnut Valley Mandolin Championship (1976-2009)
1. Ricky Rorex
2. Dave Peters
3. Robin Bullock

1995

National Flat Pick Guitar Championship
1. Mark Cosgrove
2. Cody Kilby
3. Mike Maddux

International Autoharp

Championship
1. Lucille Reilly
2. Robert T. Lewis
3. Les Gustafson-Zook

National Bluegrass Banjo Championship
1. Thomas Ivey
2. Cody Kilby
3. Randy Lucas

National Hammer Dulcimer Championship
1. Dean Lippincott
2. John Lionarons
3. Rick Thum

National Mountain Dulcimer Championship
1. Dana Hamilton
2. Tom Haver
3. Evan O'Bannon

Walnut Valley Old Time Fiddle Championship
1. John Nyen
2. Junior Marriott
3. Rainer Hagmann

National Finger Style Guitar Championship (1979-2003)
1. Pat Kirtley
2. Steve Rector
3. Jerome Arnold

Walnut Valley Mandolin Championship (1976-2009)
1. Dave Peters
2. Jason Miller
3. Bruce Graybill

1996

National Flat Pick Guitar Championship
1. Gary Cook
2. Allen Shadd
3. Cody Kilby

International Autoharp Championship
1. Robert T. Lewis
2. Tina Louise Barr
3. Alex Usher

National Bluegrass Banjo Championship
1. Gary "Biscuit" Davis
2. Randy Lucas
3. Barry Palmer

National Hammer Dulcimer Championship
1. Brenda Hunter
2. Scott Evan Freeman
3. John Lionarons

National Mountain Dulcimer Championship
1. Evan O'Bannon
2. Larry Conger
3. Jim Curley

Walnut Valley Old Time Fiddle Championship
1. Randy Howard
2. Ashley Brown
3. Jeffrey Forbes

National Finger Style Guitar Championship (1979-2003)
1. Don Ross
2. Craig Wagner
3. Eddie Rubin

Walnut Valley Mandolin Championship (1976-2009)
1. Cody Kilby
2. Randy Howard
3. Katsuyuki Miyazaki

1997

National Flat Pick Guitar Championship
1. Allen Shadd
2. Cody Kilby
3. Greg English

International Autoharp Championship
1. Karen Daniels
2. Les Gustafson-Zook
3. Drew Smith

National Bluegrass Banjo Championship
1. Randy Lucas
2. Sonny Smith
3. James McKinney

National Hammer Dulcimer Championship
1. Lucille Reilly
2. Mark Alan Wade
3. Carl Schmidt

National Mountain Dulcimer Championship
1. Hollis Landrum
2. Tom Haver

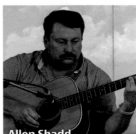

Allen Shadd

3. Jim Curley

Walnut Valley Old Time Fiddle Championship
1. Andy Leftwich
2. Matthew Palmer
3. Joel Whittinghill

National Finger Style Guitar Championship (1979-2003)
1. Todd Hallawell
2. Jalan Crossland
3. Jason Fowler

Walnut Valley Mandolin Championship (1976-2009)
1. Carlo Aonzo
2. Andy Wood
3. Joel Whittinghill

1998

National Flat Pick Guitar Championship
1. Cody Kilby
2. Carl Miner
3. Robin Kessinger

International Autoharp Championship
1. Mike Herr
2. Les Gustafson-Zook
3. Tina Louise Barr

National Bluegrass Banjo Championship
1. Sonny Smith
2. Barry Palmer
3. Cody Kilby

National Hammer Dulcimer Championship
1. Mark Alan Wade
2. Scott Evan Freeman
3. Tina Gugeler

National Mountain Dulcimer Championship

1. Larry Conger
2. Steve Eulberg
3. Mark Tindle

Walnut Valley Old Time Fiddle Championship
1. Cathy Pearson
2. Jason Shaw
3. Sandra Wong

National Finger Style Guitar Championship (1979-2003)
1. Michael Chapdelaine
2. Brad Richter
3. Sam Pacetti

Walnut Valley Mandolin Championship (1976-2009)
1. Bruce Graybill
2. Kelly Lancaster
3. Adam Wright

1999

National Flat Pick Guitar Championship
1. Carl Miner
2. Roy Curry
3. Steve Lewis

International Autoharp Championship
1. Jo Ann Smith
2. Les Gustafson-Zook
3. Alex Usher

National Bluegrass Banjo Championship
1. Charles Wood
2. Steve Lewis
3. Cody Kilby

National Hammer Dulcimer Championship
1. Scott Evan Freeman
2. Tina Gugeler
3. Samantha Oberkfell

National Mountain Dulcimer Championship
1. Lee Rowe
2. Tom Haver
3. Michael Shull

Walnut Valley Old Time Fiddle Championship
1. Alex DePue
2. Matt Cobb
3. Junior Marriott

National Finger Style

Pete Huttlinger

Guitar Championship (1979-2003)
1. Brad Richter
2. Pete Huttlinger
3. Jay Buckey

Walnut Valley Mandolin Championship (1976-2009)
1. Anthony Hannigan
2. Aco Bocina
3. Rory Ezell

2000

National Flat Pick Guitar Championship
1. Robert Shafer
2. Scott Fore
3. Jason Fowler

International Autoharp Championship
1. Drew Smith
2. Karla Armstrong
3. Les Gustafson-Zook

National Bluegrass Banjo Championship
1. Matt Menefee
2. Mike Sumner
3. Mike Swanner

National Hammer Dulcimer Championship
1. Tina Gugeler
2. Samantha Oberkfell
3. Carole Bryan

National Mountain Dulcimer Championship
1. Lloyd Frank Wright
2. Tom Haver
3. Linda Brockinton

Walnut Valley Old Time Fiddle Championship
1. Matt Cobb
2. Ross Holmes
3. Dan Kessinger

National Finger Style Guitar Championship (1979-2003)
1. Pete Huttlinger
2. Julian Smith
3. Mary Flower

Walnut Valley Mandolin Championship (1976-2009)
1. Josiah Payne
2. Charlie Provenza
3. Randy Greer

2001

National Flat Pick Guitar Championship
1. Adam Wright
2. Steve Lewis
3. Matt Lindsey

International Autoharp Championship
1. Les Gustafson-Zook
2. Alex Usher
3. Beryl Martin

National Bluegrass Banjo Championship
1. Mike Sumner
2. Steve Lewis
3. Rodney Carter

National Hammer Dulcimer Championship
1. Ben Regier
2. Joshua Messick
3. John Lionarons

National Mountain Dulcimer Championship
1. Linda Brockinton
2. Tom Haver
3. Steve Eulberg

Walnut Valley Old Time Fiddle Championship
1. Bethany Dick
2. Ross Holmes
3. Jason Shaw

National Finger Style Guitar Championship (1979-2003)
1. Richard Smith
2. Mark Anthony Cruz
3. Andy McKee

Walnut Valley Mandolin Championship (1976-2009)

1. Drew Horton
2. Robert Pearcy
3. Scott Schmidt

2002

National Flat Pick Guitar Championship
1. Scott Fore
2. Cody Frost
3. Steve Lewis

International Autoharp Championship
1. Ann Norris
2. Cathy Britell
3. Alex Usher

National Bluegrass Banjo Championship
1. John Dowling
2. Thomas Ivey
3. Steve Lewis

National Hammer Dulcimer Championship
1. Jamie Janover
2. Xiao Xiannian
3. Brenda Hunter

National Mountain Dulcimer Championship
1. Kim McKee
2. Michael Shull
3. Steve Eulberg

Walnut Valley Old Time Fiddle Championship
1. Dennis Ludiker
2. Jason Shaw
3. Ross Holmes

National Finger Style Guitar Championship (1979-2003)
1. John Standefer
2. Phil Volan
3. Bob Evans

Walnut Valley Mandolin Championship (1976-2009)
1. Scott Schmidt
2. Heidi Severin
3. Matt Raum

2003

National Flat Pick Guitar Championship
1. Jeff Troxel
2. Steve Lewis

3. Jason Shaw

International Autoharp Championship
1. Lucille Reilly
2. Cathy Britell
3. Alex Usher

National Bluegrass Banjo Championship
1. Steve Lewis
2. Eric Hardin
3. Thomas Ivey

National Hammer Dulcimer Championship
1. Joshua Messick
2. Christi Burns
3. David Mahler

National Mountain Dulcimer Championship
1. Casey Miles
2. Sue Carpenter
3. Joe Collins

Walnut Valley Old Time Fiddle Championship
1. Tashina Clarridge
2. Ross Holmes
3. Erin Tydings

National Finger Style Guitar Championship (1979-2003)
1. Bob Evans
2. Masaaki Kishibe
3. Mary Flower

Walnut Valley Mandolin Championship (1976-2009)
1. Travis Thompson
2. Scott Pearson
3. Matt Wingate

2004

National Flat Pick Guitar Championship
1. Jason Shaw
2. Matthew Arcara
3. Brandon Bentley

International Finger Style Guitar Championship
1. Keith Taylor
2. Pete Huttlinger
3. Kyle Reeder

4. International Autoharp Championship
1. Alex Usher

Jason Shaw

2. Michael Stanwood
3. Marti Knauer

National Bluegrass Banjo Championship
1. Eric Hardin
2. Clayton Cunningham
3. Jason Bales

National Hammer Dulcimer Championship
1. David Mahler
2. Princess Harris
3. Samantha Oberkfell

National Mountain Dulcimer Championship
1. Erin Rogers
2. Steve Eulberg
3. Joe Collins

Walnut Valley Old Time Fiddle Championship
1. Tristan Clarridge
2. Olivia Smiley
3. Olivia Davis

Walnut Valley Mandolin Championship (1976-2009)
1. Bruce Graybill
2. Scott Pearson
3. Matt Raum

2005

National Flat Pick Guitar Championship
1. Joe Smart
2. Tyler Grant
3. Roy Curry

International Finger Style Guitar Championship
1. Shane Adkins
2. Dan Bliss
3. Doug Smith

International Autoharp Championship

1. Cathy Britell
2. George Haig
3. Kay Stivers

National Bluegrass Banjo Championship
1. Brian Anderson
2. Jason Bales
3. Charles Wood

National Hammer Dulcimer Championship
1. Max Zbiral-Teller
2. Marvel Ang
3. Stephen Humphries

National Mountain Dulcimer Championship
1. Sue Carpenter
2. Duane Porterfield
3. Jeff Hames

Walnut Valley Old Time Fiddle Championship
1. Alex DePue
2. Olivia Smiley
3. Eric Dysart

Walnut Valley Mandolin Championship (1976-2009)
1. Jason Nelson
2. Rebecca Lovell
3. Scott Pearson

2006

National Flat Pick Guitar Championship
1. Matthew Arcara
2. Allen Shadd
3. Gary Cook

International Finger Style Guitar Championship
1. Doug Smith
2. Don Alder
3. Antoine Dufour

International Autoharp Championship
1. Doug Pratt
2. Heidi Cerigione
3. Michael Stanwood

National Bluegrass Banjo Championship
1. Charles Wood
2. Jeff Scroggins
3. Steven Moore

National Hammer Dulcimer Championship

1. Shawni Pederson
2. Cara Lindsey
3. Stephen Humphries

National Mountain Dulcimer Championship
1. Jeff Hames
2. Steve Eulberg
3. Joe Collins

Walnut Valley Old Time Fiddle Championship
1. Jake Duncan
2. James Schlender
3. Bill Jones

Walnut Valley Mandolin Championship (1976-2009)
1. Isaac Eicher
2. Brian Roe
3. Scott Pearson

2007

National Flat Pick Guitar Championship
1. Dillon Hodges
2. Carl Miner
3. Roy Curry

International Finger Style Guitar Championship
1. Don Alder
2. Tim Thompson
3. Dan Bliss

International Autoharp Championship
1. George Haig
2. Tina Louise Barr
3. Craig Harrell

National Bluegrass Banjo Championship
1. Mike Sumner
2. Jason Ericsson
3. Brett Martin

National Hammer Dulcimer Championship
1. Stephen Humphries
2. Sam Wachtler
3. Tina Gugeler

National Mountain Dulcimer Championship
1. Joe Collins
2. Robert Pearcy
3. Aaron Thornton

Walnut Valley Old Time Fiddle Championship

1. Brook Wallace
2. Ellie Goodman
3. James Schlender

Walnut Valley Mandolin Championship (1976-2009)
1. Solly Burton
2. Dominick Leslie
3. Brian Roe

2008

National Flat Pick Guitar Championship
1. Tyler Grant
2. Allen Shadd
3. Brandon Davis

International Finger Style Guitar Championship
1. Tim Thompson
2. Kyle Reeder
3. Greg Gilbertson

International Autoharp Championship
1. Craig Harrell
2. Tina Louise Barr
3. Betty Scott

National Bluegrass Banjo Championship
1. Steven Moore
2. Sonny Smith
3. Brett Martin

National Hammer Dulcimer Championship
1. Wenzhou Zhang
2. Brenda Hunter
3. Adam Sutch

National Mountain Dulcimer Championship
1. Nina Zanetti
2. Aaron Thornton
3. Jan Hammond

Walnut Valley Old Time Fiddle Championship
1. Jason Shaw
2. Marina Pendleton
3. John Shaw

Walnut Valley Mandolin Championship (1976-2009)
1. Josh Hungate
2. Josh Bailey
3. Scott Pearson

Les Gustafson-Zook

2009

National Flat Pick Guitar Championship
1. Bryan McDowell
2. Brandon Davis
3. Eric Hardin

International Finger Style Guitar Championship
1. Mark Sganga
2. Tanaka Akihiro
3. Ewan Dobson

International Autoharp Championship
1. Betty Scott
2. Rick Fitzgerald
3. Fredona Currie

National Bluegrass Banjo Championship
1. Steve Lewis
2. Ethan Waddington
3. Sonny Smith

National Hammer Dulcimer Championship
1. Linda Ferguson
2. Adam Sutch
3. Alison Coyer

National Mountain Dulcimer Championship
1. Jaekob Greene
2. Jonathan Dowell
3. Aaron Thornton

Walnut Valley Old Time Fiddle Championship
1. Bryan McDowell
2. James Schlender
3. Eric Dysart

Walnut Valley Mandolin Championship (1976-2009)
1. Bryan McDowell
2. Josh Bailey
3. Rex Preston

2010

National Flat Pick Guitar Championship
1. Jason Shaw
2. Allen Shadd
3. Andrew Hatfield

International Finger Style Guitar Championship
1. Tanaka Akihiro
2. Pete Huttlinger
3. Adam Gardino

International Autoharp Championship
1. Lucille Reilly
2. Michael Stanwood
3. Ray Choi

National Bluegrass Banjo Championship
1. Kurt Stephenson
2. Jake Workman
3. Jeremy Stephens

National Hammer Dulcimer Championship
1. Ted Yoder
2. Tina Gugeler
3. Sam Wachtler

National Mandolin Championship
1. Bryan McDowell
2. Isaac Eicher
3. Bruce Graybill

National Mountain Dulcimer Championship
1. Aaron O'Rourke
2. Bradley Ellis
3. Sarah Morgan

Walnut Valley Old Time Fiddle Championship
1. Jordan Greer
2. Alena Wheeler
3. Megan Poppe

2011

National Flat Pick Guitar Championship
1. Andrew Hatfield
2. Roy Curry
3. Allen Shadd

International Finger Style Guitar Championship
1. Kevin Horrigan
2. Kawabata Tomoaki
3. Keith Taylor

International Autoharp Championship
1. Ray Choi
2. Michael Stanwood
3. Tina Louise Barr

National Bluegrass Banjo Championship
1. Weston Stewart
2. Jake Workman
3. Paul Brown

National Hammer Dulcimer Championship
1. Tim Simek
2. Karen Alley
3. Sam Wachtler

National Mandolin Championship
1. Solly Burton
2. Peter Danzig
3. Andrew Hatfield

National Mountain Dulcimer Championship
1. Bradley Ellis
2. Evan McClanahan
3. Nathaniel Samsel

Walnut Valley Old Time Fiddle Championship
1. John Shaw
2. Emma Jane Pendleton
3. Roger Netherton

2012

National Flat Pick Guitar Championship
1. Roy Curry
2. Allen Shadd
3. Adam Wright

International Finger Style Guitar Championship
1. Adam Gardino
2. Shuhei Nishino
3. Maxwell Hughes

International Autoharp Championship
1. Michael Stanwood
2. Doug Pratt
3. Tina Louise Barr

National Bluegrass Banjo Championship
1. Gary "Biscuit" Davis
2. Kyle Tuttle
3. William Cockman

Radim Zenkl

National Hammer Dulcimer Championship
1. Matthew Dickerson
2. Nate Pultorak
3. Tina Gugeler

National Mandolin Championship
1. Jacob Jolliff
2. Andrew Hatfield
3. Gordon Neidinger

National Mountain Dulcimer Championship
1. Sarah Morgan
2. Jeff Hames
3. Michael Shull

Walnut Valley Old Time Fiddle Championship
1. Andrew Wilson
2. Roger Netherton
3. Hannah Farnum

2013

National Flat Pick Guitar Championship
1. Allen Shadd
2. Steve Kaufman
3. Matt Lindsey

International Finger Style Guitar Championship
1. Mark Anthony Cruz
2. Roger Hardin
3. Shohei Toyoda

International Autoharp Championship
1. Jo Ann Smith
2. Cindy Harris
3. Doug Pratt

National Bluegrass Banjo Championship
1. William Cockman
2. Sonny Smith
3. Kyle Tuttle

National Hammer Dulcimer Championship
1. Katie Moritz
2. Tina Gugeler
3. Nate Pultorak

National Mandolin Championship
1. Andrew Hatfield
2. Gordon Neidinger
3. J P Shafer

National Mountain Dulcimer Championship
1. Jeff Hames
2. Nathaniel Samsel
3. Jonathan Dowell

Walnut Valley Old Time Fiddle Championship
1. Katie Glassman
2. Roger Netherton
3. Kian Dye

2014

National Flat Pick Guitar Championship
1. Ben Cockman
2. Scott Fore
3. Tyler Grant

International Finger Style Guitar Championship
1. Helen Avakian
2. Hirotaka Kaneto
3. David Youngman

International Autoharp Championship
1. Bonnie Phipps
2. Cindy Harris
3. George Haig

National Bluegrass Banjo Championship
1. Brandon Green
2. Matthew Davis
3. Joey Gipson

National Hammer Dulcimer Championship
1. Karen Alley
2. Dennis Bowers
3. Nathan Graber-McCrae

National Mandolin Championship
1. Ethan Setiawan
2. Gordon Neidinger
3. David Goldenberg

National Mountain Dulcimer Championship
1. Duane Porterfield
2. Jonathan Schultes
3. Jonathan Dowell

Walnut Valley Old Time Fiddle Championship
1. Bronwyn Keith-Hynes
2. Jason Shaw
3. Roger Netherton

2015

National Flat Pick Guitar Championship
1. Scott Fore
2. Steve Kaufman
3. John Shaw

International Finger Style Guitar Championship
1. David Youngman
2. Jack Wilson
3. Lance Allen

International Autoharp Championship
1. George Haig
2. Cindy Harris
3. Marti Knauer

National Bluegrass Banjo Championship
1. Steven Moore
2. Kyle Tuttle
3. Matthew Davis

National Hammer Dulcimer Championship
1. Tina Gugeler
2. Ilace Mears
3. Kyle Paxton

National Mandolin Championship
1. David Goldenberg
2. Myles Thompson
3. Garrett Wren

National Mountain Dulcimer Championship
1. Jonathan Schultes
2. Freddy Brown
3. Daniel Worden

Walnut Valley Old Time Fiddle Championship
1. Tristan Clarridge
2. Jason Shaw
3. Regina Scott

The words that ended up scattered on these pages are a good-faith attempt to tell a story of Winfield.

They were pulled from yellowing, mouse-nibbled newspaper articles. They were told in stories shared by people who lived them.

But for every article, there are dozens more that time and critters did away with. For every story, there are thousands that could have been, should have been shared.

Memories fade, details drop by the wayside, outcomes morph into something more to our liking. Not even all the information collected for this book could make it past the unforgiving gatekeepers of space and time to be included here. At least not this time.

The problem with history is no one recognizes it as it's being made. That's as true today as it was on September 29, 1972. So, make your own history. Take time to recognize the wonder of your unique Winfield. Cherish the people you share it with. Live out the stories that get told around the campfire. Write your September's Song.

– Bob Hamrick

For Kris Wilshusen. 'You're the only tune I hear.'

Thanks to Ryan Hodgson-Rigsbee for the photos that formed the backbone of this book.

Special thanks to Bryan Masters for pulling the project off the junk heap.

· Jeff Tuttle, and all the photographers listed below
· Teri Farha
· Ted Farha
· Craig Duncan
· Camp Avalon
· Pop & The Boys and their superior others
· Mayor Rod Long
· John Harrison
· Tom Shorock
· Amy-Payne Wells
· Barry and Rene Patton
· Marilyn Taylor
· Marc Bennett and clan
· John McCutcheon
· Wendy Brynford-Jones
· Mark Noonan
· Orin Friesen, his archives and memories
· The ever-tolerant, patient residents of Winfield
· Rex Flottman and the staff of the Walnut Valley Association
· 45 years of WVF volunteers
· Everyone who is shown or mentioned on these pages

"The festival is not the performers. It's the people behind the scenes. People who often work without pay, and without getting applause every five minutes like we musicians do." *– John McCutcheon*

Photography credits

Alessandro Ravizza: 121 (right)
Austen Millkulka: 119 (right)
Bill Stephens: 18, 33
Bob Hamrick: 89 (top left)
Bryan Masters: 34-35, 116-117, 99, 128
Courtesy Alison Krauss: 124 (left)
Courtesy Byron Berline: 120
Courtesy Jason Shaw: 126 (right)
Courtesy John D. and Catherine T. MacArthur Foundation: 125 (left)
Courtesy Les Gustafson-Zook: 127 (left)
Courtesy of John McCutcheon: 4
Courtesy Peter Ostrushko: 123 (left)
Courtesy Stephen Bennett: 124 (right)
Cowboy Spencer: 78
David Firestine: 79 (bottom right)
Don Shorock: 28-29, 56 (top)
Foto Otto: 127 (right)

Gary Hamilton: 119 (left)
Jamey Firnberg: 122
Jeff Tuttle: 46-47, 48 (top right, bottom left), 49, 52 (top left, bottom center, right), 53 (top left), 63, 64, 66 (top left), 67 (bottom left, top right), 76, 86-87, 104, 106 (top left, center right), 107-109, 110 (top right, bottom left), 111, 114 (bottom right)
Joe Tholen: 67 (top left)
Marty O'Sullivan: 12, 13 (left, bottom right)
Michael Cobb: 53 (bottom right), 67 (bottom right)
Mitch Weiss: 123 (right)
Paul Schatzkin: 126 (left)
Richard Crowson, Wichita Eagle: 10
Ron Shufflebarger: 118, 65 (bottom right), 67 (center right), 52 (top center, bottom left), 66 (top right, bottom right)
Russell A. Cothren: 21

Russell Lambrestche: 65 (top right)
Ryan Hodgson-Rigsbee: 2-3, 19, 22, 24-27, 30-32, 36-39, 42-45, 48 (top left, bottom right), 50-51, 52 (center left, center), 53 (top left-center, top right-center, top right, left bottom, right-center bottom, right center), 54-55, 56 (bottom), 57-61, 62 (left), 66 (center right), 68-75, 77, 79 (top right), 80-85, 88, 89 (bottom left, top center, top right, center, bottom center, bottom right), 90-98, 100-103, 105, 106 (top center, top right, center left, bottom left, bottom right), 110 (top left, bottom right), 112-113, 114 (top left, bottom left), 115
Southwestern College: 5-6
Steve Adelson: 89 (center left)
Steve Gerig: 40-41, 13 (top right)
Tom Shorock: 117
Walnut Valley Association: 8,9, 11, 14-17, 20, 125 (right)

Bob Hamrick is a professional writer and amateur musician from Wichita, Kansas.

Working as a marketing copywriter, Bob has received numerous professional honors, including three Emmy awards. He is author of the book, "Looking Back, Moving Forward: A Story of Wichita's Old Town."

A long-time devotee of the Walnut Valley Festival, Bob remembers his first Land Rush. "I buried my '76 VW bus up to the axle in mud. As I started digging out, the first thing I saw was a bumper sticker left by the previous owner: 'I got stuck in paradise.' I took it as a sign."

In 2004, Bob and his squeezebox joined Pop & The Boys. The band has often played Winfield's Stage 5, as well as the annual Bluegrass Walkabout. In 2015, the group joined Barry Patton and Byron Berline for a Stage 2 performance.

Bob and wife Kris Wilshusen's family includes daughter, Marlo Hamrick, an attorney for Kansas Legal Services, and daughter-in-law Shannon Knipp.